DISCARDED

What America Means to Me

What America Means to Me

PEARL S. BUCK

Essay Index Reprint Series

BOOKS FOR LIBRARIES PRESS
FREEPORT, NEW YORK

Copyright 1942, 1943 by Pearl S. Buck

Copyright © renewed 1970
by Pearl S. Buck

Reprinted 1971 by arrangement with
The John Day Company, Inc.

INTERNATIONAL STANDARD BOOK NUMBER:
0-8369-2387-1

LIBRARY OF CONGRESS CATALOG CARD NUMBER:
79-156622

PRINTED IN THE UNITED STATES OF AMERICA
BY
NEW WORLD BOOK MANUFACTURING CO., INC.
HALLANDALE, FLORIDA 33009

CONTENTS

	Introduction	v
1.	The Dark Shadow	1
2.	East and West	9
3.	Equality	20
4.	Freedom	38
5.	The Meaning of India	51
6.	China Faces the Future	67
7.	Relief—for the American Conscience	87
8.	The Spirit Behind the Weapon	94
9.	The Changing War	107
10.	Not Quite Too Late	117
11.	Can the Church Lead?	126
12.	Children and the World	135
13.	To Win the Peace	154
14.	Can the English Trust Us?	170

15.	Two Americans
	    I. Thomas Jefferson
	    II. Abraham Lincoln
		181

16.	What America Means to Me	196

INTRODUCTION

In the midst of the war there is beginning to grow something new in the hearts of the peoples of all nations. The peoples are impatient for the war to be ended because they feel something new is ahead, an experience which they are eager to begin. What it is none knows, for the stirring of rebirth is not yet a knowledge so much as it is an instinct. Victory for the peoples in this war is necessary, for the peoples must be free or the rebirth will not come. Every era of renaissance has come out of new freedoms for peoples. The coming renaissance will be greater than any in human history, for this time all the peoples of the earth will share in it. Freedom for all must be the principle of the peace that the atmosphere may be right for the full flowering of this rebirth.

What has led us to this moment?

First, the development of science—science applied to swift ships, to airplanes, to motor vehicles of every kind; science, building new roads in all the countries, brought the peoples closer, not only the peoples of different countries but the people within the limits of a single nation. In China the people of different provinces were as alien as though they lived in separate nations until steamships on the rivers and motor vehicles on new roads, brought

An article in *Asia and the Americas*, June, 1943.

INTRODUCTION

them face to face. In Africa, in South America, in Russia, people are living through the same experience of learning to know their own countrymen. But ships and airplanes have tied the continents together, too, and have bridged the nations.

Second came the war to hasten the process of acquaintance. It might have taken another century to do what the war has done in a few years. The war has forced peoples together as allies or enemies. The peoples of China and America and Britain have been compelled to know the peoples of Japan and Germany from an evil experience, but they have been compelled to know them. The peoples of China and America have been forced to new knowledge of each other as allies. Russia's people, too, have had to be known anew. But it is a hasty and incomplete knowledge, this knowledge which war has forced upon the peoples. It is like a short course in college, taken under the compulsion of an examination. There is no depth to it. The abnormal unhealthy experience of war has only given them glimpses of each other fighting, in deep distress, wounded, dying. The peoples have not had the experience yet of living together.

But the war has done this, at least—it has created a desire among peoples for further knowledge. The peoples of the United Nations look toward each other with new interest and wonder and hope. Having fought side by side to victory, they are asking, what then, can we not carry on this relationship in times of peace? It is out of this wonder and this hope that the rebirth will come, the new Renaissance, the greatest that mankind has yet known.

Any new birth comes from a cooperative process, a fertilizing and a fostering. The Renaissance of the Mid-

INTRODUCTION

dle Ages in Europe came from such cooperation. The age preceding it had been a sterile one, in spite of Europe's riches. Something was lacking, something new to inspire and energize. The opening of routes to the East provided the stimulus. The rich soil of Europe was impregnated with new knowledge from the East, and out of the union there came such a flowering of the human mind that men have looked back to it with wonder ever since. The imagination of the peoples of Europe was stirred, they woke and began to create new arts and new crafts, to undertake new industries and to shape a new life which penetrated into every phase of society. No one escaped the benefits of the Renaissance.

In that age it was the peoples of the East who gave it to the peoples of the West. The East was not stirred in return. The life of the eastern peoples was already rich, so much richer than that of Europe that they could give out of their abundance of culture and learning and achievement, and feel no need of return.

But there was still no real communication between the peoples. The life of the world, East and West, went on, separated by seas and distance. The impetus given to Europe continued to flower over a long period and spread to the American hemisphere. Now it was Asia that grew sterile with age and isolation, and now it was the West's turn to impregnate the East.

The rebirth came to the East when steamships were invented. Ships went to China and to India and to Japan in numbers greater than ever before, carrying traders and missionaries and diplomats. The East was unwilling and unresponsive in those days. The peoples of China and Japan and India did not want to be disturbed. They had lived in their own silence so long, and the new-

INTRODUCTION

comers were noisy and boisterous and arrogant. Yet what the eastern peoples did not welcome they had to accept. Life forced them into life again, however unwillingly.

But all birth is unwilling. The child in the womb struggles against being born. The old, accustomed to age, struggle against death, the new form of life. Thus rebirth came to the East and the peoples woke and began to live in the modern world, a world full of conflicts and wars, but alive. Revolutions in China and in Russia, unrest and discontent in India, an angry militarism in Japan, these have been the signs of awaking peoples of the East.

Now world war has thrown the doors open wide. We know that when the war is won there will be no more barriers of sea and distance between us. We know that swifter ships and more ships than ever before will be daily, hourly, crossing the seas. We know that in the skies the great airplanes will be speeding from people to people. Already those who build the airplanes are beginning to quarrel over the air routes—as though the skies belonged to any, and not to all!

The peoples, still in the throes of this most bitter war, are looking ahead and seeing and feeling the possibilities of all that can be, if there is freedom for it to be. Communication between them, travel quick and cheap, the interchange of the treasures of merchandise, of new flowers and plants and trees, the even more important exchange of thoughts and new ways, the pooling of that which human beings have learned in the centuries lived apart—all this the peoples are already thinking about or imagining.

This rebirth will be the greatest of all, for there is more equality now between the peoples than there has

INTRODUCTION

ever been before. In the Renaissance of the Middle Ages it was the East that gave to the West. In the modern renaissance of Asia it was the West that gave to the East. But now each has something to give to the other, and from this mutual need and mutual richness there will spring, if the times are free, life for mankind richer and better than anything we have yet known.

What has the West to give the East? A better physical life, a practical knowledge of medicine and hygiene and of all the ways in which science can improve health and environment, an improved industrial life, industries which are the creation of science applied to man's needs for work and for finished materials and for the objects he uses every day for convenience and pleasure. Most important of all, the West can give the East a technique of modern democracy, which provides for the individual a method of expressing his own opinion and wielding his own power in the government of his people.

What has the East to give the West? Deep knowledge of how people can live together happily and with mutual respect, the Chinese philosophy of reasonableness so practically applied by China's people for ages, and the value of the individual human spirit which has been its fruit; the deep belief in man's relation to God and eternity, that belief in which the peoples of India live and move and have their being, and the noble patience which has been the fruit of it; the loyalty and high sense of duty which the people of Japan have developed, even when the object of that loyalty has been unworthy; the conviction of the equality of all races upon which Russia alone out of all the peoples has founded her new nation.

We of the West need spiritual enrichment today as never before. In our preoccupation with the wonders of

INTRODUCTION

science applied to materials we have forgotten that man does not live by bread alone. These words came out of the East two thousand years ago and it is the people of the East who have never forgotten them and who must teach us again their truth.

East and West, today the peoples need each other. Nothing must be allowed to keep us apart, neither the greed of merchants nor the prejudices of the arrogant. The plain peoples of the earth must find each other, they must discover that they are alike in their simple and deep desires. East and West, we do long for the same things, for love and home and children, for work whose fruit will feed the family; for peace, for freedom in which to live and think and grow. These are not impossible longings, not dreams that cannot be realized. They are the rights of all mankind. But the plain peoples must work together to achieve them, and give them to each other, or they will not have them. And how can they work together except as they cease to be strangers and become friends?

It is the duty of all, therefore, to open every door of approach, to cultivate every source of knowledge, to try to find out by any means possible, the ways and habits and beliefs and hopes of other peoples not their own, to the end that with common knowledge and in mutual understanding, all peoples may work together for a good and peaceful world.

WHAT AMERICA MEANS TO ME

1. THE DARK SHADOW

"Come in, please," a young girl's soft voice said, "Mother is expecting you."

The young girl was very pretty, I saw that at my first glance. She was dark, eyes black, and her black hair smoothly curled and shining. If she had been born in Samoa or in the Philippines, she would have been called an island beauty. But she was born in the United States of America, in the city of Philadelphia.

She wore a white dress, plain and smart, and as she led the way into the quiet house that stood on a quiet street, I saw she had that peculiar grace which one sees so often in the South Seas. But there was nothing foreign about her when she talked. Her speech was pure American.

"Will you please come upstairs?" she said.

So I followed her upstairs into a dignified and even handsome room, where we sat down while we waited for her mother.

"Mother is talking to my grandmother," she said. "Grandmother has just had a long distance call from my father—because it is Mother's Day, you know! My father is a major in the army, a doctor, with the new flying corps of Tuskegee."

She was proud of her father, I could see that. But I could imagine any father being proud, too, of this daughter, so graceful, so full of ease and poise even with a stranger.

"This child," I thought, watching her and listening as she answered my questions about her school life, "is a happy child."

She told me that she went to a public school where colored and white girls mingled together without self-consciousness. She liked her friends, she said, and had a good time and she was not often treated differently because she was not white. But as she said this I saw a little shadow in the really beautiful dark eyes. I put a question to that shadow.

"Don't your colored schoolmates ever feel any disadvantage in not being white?"

Yes, it seemed they did, especially when they were seniors. There had long been a pleasant custom in the school that the senior class went before it was graduated on a trip to Washington, the capital of their country. It was meant as a sort of climax to their years of education in the excellent public school. Actually it was anti-climax and contradiction to what they had been taught. For the colored girls could not go because they would not be admitted to the hotels with their schoolmates. There was no hotel in Washington which would take the girls if some of them were colored.

"So the white girls go and we don't," this child said quietly. She added hastily. "Of course we want them to go—we wouldn't want them to miss the fun—just because we must."

"I should like you to know," I said, "that if I were a white girl in your school I wouldn't go if you could not. I am ashamed of those white girls who go without you to visit Washington, of all places."

THE DARK SHADOW

She did not answer this, but she smiled a painful little smile.

"It won't be a problem this year, anyway," she said. "We can't any of us go because of the war."

Her mother came in then, a woman graceful and pretty enough to explain her daughter. She was a quiet woman, gentle with long breeding.

"How long have you been in Philadelphia?" I asked when we began to talk.

She had been born in Philadelphia, and her family had been here for three generations. That is, she was of an old American family. The generation earlier had been in the South. A white ancestor had brought them here.

I suspected several white ancestors in this beautiful woman. Her skin was golden brown, and her hair was smooth and her features fine.

"Tell me," I said, "you are of very mixed blood?"

She told me frankly then of the story of those generations. Except for the mixed blood it might have been the story of any old and honorable American family whose ancestors had come here early and had lived in dignity and even some luxury. Obviously this woman had never known want or insecurity. Her husband, too, had a mixture, white blood from Lancaster county in Pennsylvania, where the Pennsylvania Dutch have no race prejudices.

"Here is his picture," she said. I looked into the face of a handsome and strong man. He wore a uniform.

"He fought in the last war, too," she said proudly, "and he didn't feel he was doing his duty until he volunteered again. But I hope he'll get home before he has to go abroad."

WHAT AMERICA MEANS TO ME

The house was very quiet. As she said this, I felt the quietness began in her.

"Are you two quite alone here now?" I asked.

Yes, it seemed they were. There was an older daughter away at college living in a dormitory, I learned, with white girls. I asked to see her picture, too, and they brought me another framed photograph. I looked into an extremely fair and pretty face.

"What a handsome family you are!" I exclaimed.

They smiled at that, but as if they had heard it before.

We had tea, and we talked and I heard of the trip to Europe where the father had gone for advanced study in medicine. Why had he gone to Europe, I asked?

The faint shadow passed over the pretty woman's face. "It's easier for us over there," she said. Then she added, "We doubted whether he would have been allowed to do the same work here."

Until then I had been enjoying myself. I had been thinking, here is a colored American family who feels no disadvantage in their color. Obviously they are well-to-do, highly educated, and happy. I had never had this experience before. I had not seen colored Americans who did not have a rankling bitter sense of injustice done them. This family, I thought with relief, showed that it was possible to live in America, colored, and yet like anyone else.

"Does your husband have white patients as well as colored?" I asked.

"Oh, yes," the pretty woman said. "He goes wherever he is needed."

"And you," I asked, "do you have white friends?"

"No," she said quietly, "I have none."

THE DARK SHADOW

"But your daughter," I persisted, "she tells me she goes to school with white girls?"

"So did I," the mother said, "but after school I didn't see them any more."

"But why?" I asked.

"One doesn't want to go where the welcome is doubtful," she replied.

The shadow was very clear now. I determined to pierce it and find out what it meant.

"Let's talk frankly about this matter of race," I said. "Do you have much trouble with it here in Philadelphia?"

"Oh, no," she said quickly. "Not if we choose our places. That is, there are nice places to eat where they will let us come in and we just don't go to the other places. We soon find out where the right places are and we avoid—insult."

"And the theatres?"

"The best ones don't discriminate," she said. "And we can hear good music—they let us come to the concerts."

"They?" I asked.

"The white people," she said, gently. .

"But you have your own friends?" I asked.

"Oh, yes," she said. Her face brightened. "I have very nice friends, and their daughters are my daughter's friends. We have a pleasant little set of our own and we live within it."

We talked on for an hour more, I pressing my questions and she answering with a sort of sweet frankness that I found charming. Now and again the dark pretty daughter would add something.

I began after a while to have strange twinges of memory. Where had I seen this sort of thing before—delicate pretty women, sensitive faces, well-bred manners and gentle voices, interest in music and theatre, and yet all of it hedged about with an unexpressed fear? Where before had I seen this world within a world? While we talked I let my mind go searching into the past, until I found the people of whom these two women reminded me.

What I remembered were the refugees in many parts of the world. They were the families of white Russian noblemen in Shanghai, driven out of their own country by the communists. In a drawing room in Shanghai I had sat sometimes like this, listening to Russian ladies who were living in a little world of their own, trying to forget the real world. Yes, and I remembered refugees in France, the early refugees from Germany, well-born, well-bred people, living in a small circle, maintaining their life by forgetting what they did not want to remember. And the other day in New York I saw the refugees again, Chinese ladies in New York, ladies from Hong Kong and Shanghai, from Hangchow and Peking, come to America, infinitely strange here in their delicacy and their beauty, clinging together, trying to make a little world for themselves in a fearful world outside.

Yes, that is what they reminded me of, this American mother and daughter.

"Do you feel American?" I asked suddenly. They were startled by the question. "Oh, yes," the mother said. It was her first touch of real passion. "Why," she said, "we belong here!"

She looked at me, bewildered, I could see, by my question, and half-frightened by it. "We've been here for generations," she said, "and my husband's fighting for America. Oh, yes, we're American."

THE DARK SHADOW

But now the shadow was very dark indeed, so dark that I had not the heart to go on trying to pierce it. Besides, I understood it. Remembering the refugees had made me understand. We talked only a few minutes more after that, about small things, and I came away. When I shut the door it was like shutting it on a walled garden, beautiful but enclosed, and the gate was locked behind me.

I came away carrying the shadow with me. Think of living in your own country, but having to be watchful continually for insult! Think of being sensitive and intelligent, educated and gently bred, and having to pause at the door of a hotel, at a restaurant, at the door of a railway car, at a theatre, at a store—everywhere, that is—and to ask yourself "Will they let me come in here? Or will they tell me they don't want us?"

Thinking myself into those two with whom I had spent the afternoon, I began to share that shadow. What misery to live forever anticipating the insult, forever dreading the rebuff! And for nothing except the faint golden tinge to the skin! For these two women were the equals of any I had met in any country and superior to many I knew of my own race. For myself I was proud that they were Americans. I was bitterly ashamed of the shadow over their lives.

"Have you ever been to Virginia?" I had asked them thoughtlessly.

"Never!" the mother had answered quickly.

"We never go south," the daughter had said proudly.

And I know why. Were I they, I, too, would never go south.

A good many days have passed since I spent my afternoon in that quiet house. But the shadow I brought

WHAT AMERICA MEANS TO ME

away from it is with me still. I think it will be with me as long as it is here in our country, for race prejudice is not only a shadow over the colored—it is a shadow over all of us, and the shadow is darkest over those who feel it least and allow its evil effects to go on. It is not healthy when a nation lives within a nation, as colored Americans are living inside America. A nation cannot live confident of its tomorrow if its refugees are among its own citizens.

For it is never the one who suffers injustice who is the injured one, but the one who is unjust. Slavery bred a race of idle and shiftless white men, and race prejudice continues the evil work. White people who insist on their superiority because of the color of the skin they were born with—can there be so empty and false a superiority as this? Who is injured the most by that foolish assumption, the colored or the white? In his soul it is the white man.

It is the wise white people who ought now to be angry because of race prejudice, for as surely as night follows day our country will fail in its democracy because of race prejudice unless we root it out. We cannot grow in strength and leadership for democracy so long as we carry deep in our being this fatal fault. It is the white people who are endangered by race prejudice. We are endangered in the world, where there are many millions more of colored people than of white. The world will close down on us some day if race prejudice goes on dividing us.

Where are those who will see our danger? Where are those who will move swiftly to save us before it is too late?

2. EAST AND WEST

WHEN one contemplates the world in which we live today, one is reminded of that puzzling toy —I am afraid it was made in Japan—which came in the form of a wooden egg. When this egg was opened there was another egg inside and when this was opened another and yet another, down to the last center egg. This last egg, if I remember my childhood correctly, could not be opened. It was solid and compact, and there it was, simply an end, not an answer.

So in viewing the immensity of war as it is taking place at this moment, it seems too complicated, not only in space as it covers the earth, but even more in the time it covers into the possible future. Hitler may be driven off Russian soil this year but will that end the war even for Russia? Where is the end of this war? It seems to me that to drive Hitler off Russian soil is merely to open the first egg. Inside there is another.

The second egg may be the defeat of Hitler in Europe. That, too, is possible, perhaps, within the visible future. But that, too, is simply another egg. Inside there is another. It is the problem of Japan, victorious at this moment in Asia on a scale beyond the imagination, perhaps,

An article published substantially in this form in *The New York Times Magazine*, May 31, 1942.

even of herself. It is not necessary to recount what she now holds, if she does not yet possess it all. There is, of course, a difference between what one seizes and what one really possesses. It will take time for Japan to take possession of what she has won by war. But unfortunately the genius of Japan lies in her ability to organize as she organized Formosa, Korea and Manchuria, and as she has organized in a fashion even occupied China in spite of guerrillas and brave resistance from the Chinese.

One can open several eggs on this matter of Japan. Why was she able to move so quickly and easily over territory long possessed by England and Holland? The plain fact of the matter is, and the sooner we realize it the better, that too many of the people of the East have not helped the people of the West in this war. The white man has been fighting a desperate and in many parts of Asia a hopeless war, and he has been afraid to tell how desperate and hopeless it is. We have had hints through the newspapers but only hints. If we cannot know how much the Japanese have been aided, at least we may be sure of this—that if the allies had been fully aided, Japan could have won no territory whatever. It is idle to say that "we" have been outnumbered. We would not have been outnumbered if the people on whose soil we have been fighting had helped us with their main force of resistance.

Here is the central hard solid egg in the heart of all this war in the East. We had better take it out and look at it, and face what it means. This Second World War has taken on a new and dangerous aspect, most of all because of Japan. Although we may not be willing to know it, it is possible that we are already embarked upon the bitterest and the longest of human wars, the war between the East and the West, and this means the war between the white man and his world and the colored man and his world. The greatest danger is not only that today Japan is in a position of unprecedented strength, but that Japan is an Asiatic power, and whatever her despotism, she stands to millions of Asiatics for freedom at least from the white man's despotism. To know what that means to the average man in the East, you have only to ask any ordinary white man in the West if he would rather have a yellow man or a white man rule over him, regardless of their rule, and you will get the average answer—he would rather have his own kind. I think that no Asian has any illusion about the tyranny of Japan, but he feels that at least it will be a tyranny not made more intolerable by a difference of race which the white man historically has used for his own advantage.

Can the white man and the colored man ever come together in any sort of cooperation? That is the crux of the future. In the answer to that question is the answer to where and when this war will end. A truce which does not take into account the question and the answer will be only a temporary breathing space for recuperation for yet a greater phase of the war. If Americans deny the question and evade the answer, if they ignore it as a matter of policy and diplomacy, it is simply to behave like the ostrich, because in Asia no one denies it or evades it. In India it is the burning question, whose flames leap higher every hour, in Burma it is a raging fire, in Java, yes, and in the Philippines and in China. For while the Filipino has fought well beside the white man, it is only because he has had his promise of freedom from him. If China is still heroically with us against

Japan, she is, like Russia, fighting for herself and her own life, and she will be the first to demand her own complete freedom even from those who are now her allies. For white men to try to escape the blaze in Asia which this war has set free may be to end in the fire which they are as yet doing little to put out.

The main barrier between East and West today is that the white man is not willing to give up his superiority and the colored man is no longer willing to endure his inferiority.

To gauge the full difference in the point of view one has only to listen to a group of Indians or Chinese or Koreans or Filipinos talking freely among themselves about the white people, and to listen to a group of Americans or English talking among themselves about these others. The white man is a century behind the colored man. The white man is still thinking in terms of colonies and the colonial government. The colored man knows that colonies and colonial-mindedness are anachronisms. The colonial way of life is over whether the white man knows it or not, and all that remains is to kick off the shell of the chrysalis. The man of Asia today is not a colonial and he has made up his mind he will never be a colonial again.

I wish it were possible to avoid this discussion of color. I wish it were possible to be a pure idealist and to speak of people as human beings, some of whom care for other human beings and some of whom do not. The only real division among us all is of character and not of skin. There are good and bad, selfish and unselfish, honest and dishonest, inside of all skins. But so long as the color of a skin and not character is what decides a man's status, social and economic, then it is idle to refuse to recognize the fact of race. So long as white men in America will not sit in the same car with colored men, so long as in India a drop of Indian blood makes a man colored and not white, so long as being Chinese makes it impossible for a sailor to get shore-leave in the port of New York, then we must conclude that race does matter more than anything else. By all practical tests race is certainly the most dividing barrier between East and West. To deny it is subterfuge.

Can this barrier be destroyed?

If it cannot then we must prepare for a future of nothing but struggle and war on a stupendous scale, particularly for the white man. We shall have to make up for our inferiority in numbers by military preparation of the most barbarous and savage kind. We must prepare super-weapons, we must not shrink from chemical warfare on a mass scale, we must be willing to destroy all civilization, even our own, in order to keep down the colored peoples who are so vastly our superior in numbers and our equal in skills. Is this a future which any human being wants to face?

I cannot think it is. And yet it is a possible future. It may be, I think, an inevitable one, unless we are willing to take every step to prevent it. It is not the old cry of the Yellow Peril. This is not a peril unless peoples who are determined on freedom and human equality are denied them. There is in a sense a White Peril or a Black Peril or a Soil Erosion Peril or a Plague Peril or any other kind of peril in the world if we take no steps to prevent perils.

But before we consider steps, let us consider our assets in this war of the peoples.

First and greatest of all our assets is the fact that we

have the Chinese on the same side with us, because we are fighting Japan. We ought to make the most of the Chinese as our allies, because their very presence at our side cuts across the dangerous division of Race. Have we made the most of China as an ally? No, certainly we have not. One needs only to mention a few facts haphazardly. Americans must remember the shipping of war materials to Japan, and we ought to remember the continued exclusion of Chinese from our shores and as citizens; this would be a singularly appropriate moment to modify our exclusion laws against Chinese. We ought to know, too, of such things as the ignorance of some officers in our ports which the other day in New York resulted in insult to a high Chinese official when he went in the course of his duty to look after his own national who happened to be a witness to the murder of a Chinese sailor by a British captain. We ought to know of the refusal in Mississippi, and it may be in other states, to allow Chinese children to go to school with white children. The list of facts which we ought to know could go on and on. Be sure these facts are known everywhere in Asia if not in our own country, and they neutralize for us the asset of China.

And our British allies ought to know of the ways in which they, too, are not using the asset that China is to us. I will mention only two which had serious effect upon the war in Burma. Chinese soldiers were long massed on the Chinese border, impatient to fight in Burma, but they were not allowed to cross over and take their part until Rangoon fell and it became obvious that the British alone could not hold the ground. Again, as soon as General Stilwell was appointed to head the Chinese armies, a British general was advanced to superior rank. I do not pretend to know anything about the military reasons for this. But I do know that the effect upon our Chinese allies was unfortunate. Much will be told one day of the treatment of the Chinese and others in the allied retreats from Malaya and Burma. To remove our ignorance of such facts would be one of the first steps toward using to the full our great assets of China in our war in the Pacific. It is China alone who is contradicting by her very presence at our side the Japanese propaganda that Britain and America will never cooperate with colored races. We ought to give China every advantage—she is worth far more to us at this moment than her weight in future trade and gold. She may be the one country some day which will prevent the war of East against West. But China needs reassurance and quick reassurance of her complete human equality in the mind of the white man.

We have another asset, and it is in the colored people of the United States. We Americans are singularly fortunate, if we only knew it, in having ten percent of our people colored. It gives Americans a chance to get ready for the future. If we can work out a cooperation, here and now, on equal terms between colored and white, we shall be more ready for the future than we possibly could be if our colored people lived as far away from us, say, as India is from England. We have a unique chance to destroy a good deal of the barrier between white and colored by doing it here in our own country. The loyalty of the colored Americans, their high character as individuals in spite of long and crushing disadvantages, is amazing to one who comes upon them with fresh eyes.

We have an asset in the people of India, too. It is unwise when Americans today say that India is not our business, dangerous when we gloat over the imprisonment and death of Indian patriots. Too many shortsighted Americans say "Britain owns India, Britain is our ally, it would be silly to interfere with India." Silly for the short present, perhaps, but very wise for the long future! The truth is that India has become the business of the Allies and is no longer the possession of any country. Our American soldiers are being sent there in unknown numbers. They can go as soldiers of empire or as soldiers of freedom—these are the two alternatives. If we cannot prove to India that our soldiers are there for freedom, then India will believe they are there for empire.

Is this anti-British? No, in the truest sense it is pro-British, for in England, too, there are many who believe this and who speak out their belief with urgency. When we in America speak for justice and fairness toward India we are not lonely voices—English voices are speaking the same words with greater fervor. India can be a great asset to our allied cause if we are wise enough to use her. But we are losing our best chances when we encourage the attitude which has given full attention only to the imperial point of view toward India, modified and enlightened even as it was in Sir Stafford Cripps, and when we deny equal attention to the statements of Indian leaders giving Indian points of view. We are losing our chances with India when we allow the slighting comments of ignorant radio speakers and newspaper columnists to go unchallenged—comments, for instance, which lump together all Moslems, as though the All-India Congress did not represent Moslems too, as though the very president of the Congress were not himself a Moslem, or comments which deny the so-called "paci-

EAST AND WEST

fism" of India, which is not pacifism at all, but the brave determination of a people to resist Japan in the way they know best, since arms have not been allowed to them. Our ignorance of India is playing straight into Japan's hands and Hitler's. We must for our own sakes try to understand India now. To condemn without understanding is too dangerous for us.

Our allied cause has another asset in the Filipinos. It may be that one day their voices will be raised for the white man because once white men treated them with goodness, and promised them their freedom and gave them a date for it.

We have another asset in the Koreans, a people long and cruelly subject to Japan, and now eagerly looking forward to their independence when allied victory becomes a fact. If we could make them know that their independence is truly a part of our allied cause, a promise to be kept, we could mobilize to our side the millions of Korea. Who could speak to Asia more eloquently than these of the tyranny of Japan?

And there is the great asset of Russia, a nation partly East and partly West, a nation whose new life is founded upon racial equality—will the Russians stay with the West if the people of the West will not accept human equality?

If we are honest, we must admit that we are wasting these assets, for the most part, when we still try to maintain our outworn standards of the superiority of the white man in the world as it once was. We do not know what has been happening among the colored peoples while we have been enjoying our superiority, nor what has already happened, beyond revoke.

In the given situation, then, can the barrier between

East and West be broken down? I should say, if attitudes remain unchanged, no, the barrier will not only not be broken down but it will grow higher and higher and the end will be a war between East and West, in which the Chinese will not be on our side. Asia is determined to have freedom.

Can our attitude be changed? Yes, but only first by unprejudiced information which will lighten our present general dense ignorance about Asia, and then by concentrated determination to hew out our course not according to past lines of race and empire but along new lines of common humanity and cooperative equality.

How can this be done? It can be done only by a powerful determination among people in America to know for themselves how people in Asia feel and what they want and why they want it. There must be a further mutual determination for real human equality, discarding race as a basis for discrimination.

I have purposely put the main responsibility for change upon the West, for the fact is, as those of the white race know who have lived intimately among the peoples of Asia, that race prejudice is not to be found in Asia in the discriminatory form in which it is found in the West. It is natural anywhere that people like their own kind, but it is not necessarily natural that their fondness for their own kind should lead them to the subjection of whole groups of other people not like them.

Why should the white man have so generally denied human equality to the colored man? It is not that the white man is inherently evil or the colored man inherently good. Individual character runs about the same in any group. No, the white man has happened to hold the

EAST AND WEST

power largely through his inventive skill in science. Science has been his genius and now it may be his undoing. For the force of his scientific knowledge has expressed itself mainly in materials and warfare. But the peoples of the East at the same time have been developing knowledge of human relations and hatred of war. It has actually been more important to the man of the East to discover how to live amicably with his neighbor than it has been to devise a gun with which to kill his neighbor. The extremes of East and West are fundamentally to be found in the extremes between a man who thinks most highly of life and how to live it, and of the man who thinks most highly of war and how to wage it. The two extremes are perhaps equally impractical. A gun is a handy thing at times, but life is useless when it is destroyed.

But the man in the East is leaving his extreme and is beginning to finger a gun, too. If the white man does not now save himself by discovering that all men are really born free and equal, he may not be able to save himself at all. For the colored man is going to insist on that human equality and that freedom.

The tragic aspect of the whole matter is that the barrier between East and West is an artificial one. If race could be put aside, and if people could consider people on the basis of simple humanity, there would be no barrier. The peoples of India and China believe this, and they look to America with intense and questioning hope. Can America see the potentiality of this moment? An outspoken declaration, a practical act, to prove our belief in human equality and our conviction of the necessity of freedom as a right for all, and East would be one with West today.

3. EQUALITY

THESE are not ordinary times, and this is no ordinary graduating class. Today the individual has to contribute to the human demand of our times or he misses too much. Today you are not only a group of individuals beginning your individual lives in a country which is more or less of a democracy. You are a specially privileged group, not even because of the education which you have begun here under such excellent circumstances. But you are privileged because at this moment in human history you are a group with a special opportunity and a special duty to the times which none but you can perform, and this because of what you have been born, as well as because of what you have received.

Let us review your situation at this moment. You are Americans. You are Americans of old families and not of recent immigration. This means that for some generations your families have lived in a country which has believed in democracy and freedom of the individual even if it has not practiced human equality. You belong somewhere near the top of your group or you would not be here today, at a Commencement at a good university. You have been accustomed to some financial security,

Commencement address at Howard University, Washington, June 5, 1942.

EQUALITY

and certainly to some intellectual background or you would not have considered it worth while to spend the time and the effort and the money on a university education. Obviously, you are well above the average of all Americans.

And yet I know that I would not be saying anything worth saying if I did not speak of what I know also to be true—that in the heart of every one of you, whether you talk about it or not, there is doubt, not about yourselves, but about your place in society. It is only inevitable that many, if not all of you, are asking how much you can actually accomplish, even with your unusual equipment, and how relentlessly the barriers of race prejudice in your country will hold you back.

I know that some of you by carefully living in a world within a world can perhaps manage fairly well, in a limited way, to make a life. There is a way in which you can live which avoids the area of race prejudice almost entirely, and which within the circumscribed area of a small nation subject to a larger one, can give you reasonable security. Those of you who tend naturally to retreat into security will probably choose that world. Who can blame you if you do? There has been nothing to encourage you to break down the walls which race prejudice puts about you, and it has been individual wisdom, perhaps, to live within the walls rather than to waste one's self and spend one's energies in trying to break down what has been until now a relentless barrier.

I will confess that I have been completely perplexed by this race prejudice in my own country. Having lived always until eight years ago in China, where there is almost no race prejudice as such, I did not know my own country in this regard. Even my four years in college in a southern town did not teach me the full meaning of it. College in my day and especially for young women was a limiting and not an enlarging experience. I had come from a larger place into a smaller one when I came here to college and I went back to China immediately when I had finished.

It was only when I returned to my own country to live that I became aware of the amazing fact that Americans were actually divided into two parts, and that the two parts were living as though they were two separate nations, except that they had the same government. This seemed to me a very alarming and dangerous situation in a democracy and I at once began to inquire into it. I listened to both colored and white Americans talk and explain their points of view and their experiences of each other, and the division grew deeper daily as I came to understand the full reality of race prejudice and its effect upon both colored and white people.

Without an emergency to quicken a social change, what could be done? I tried to think as one of the minority—not difficult, because in China I had all my life belonged to a minority race—there the white race—and as a white, in spite of my very close relations and even integration into Chinese life, I had suffered some of the inevitable experiences of those who are in the minority in any country. But I had to think newly. What, I asked myself, would I do if I belonged to a group in my own country against which race prejudice worked?

I remember one of the first things I thought I would do would be to devote myself to the development of all superior colored children. Obviously the colored people lack leadership. We hark back too much to people who are dead. Crispus Attucks, hero that he was, is dead. So

EQUALITY

is Booker Washington and so is Harriet Tubman. We need living heroes of our people. I remember how forcibly this was once brought to my attention in an essay contest for colored students of which I was one of the judges. In many scores of essays the students, both high school and college, mentioned the same half dozen heroes of their people. Almost the only one then living was Dr. Carver. Now I know Dr. Carver's work and have heard him talk about it and I agree to his greatness as a scientist. But one living great man is not enough for any people. We might add, I think, Paul Robeson, and we might put at his side Dorothy Maynor and Marian Anderson, as great in their peculiar gifts and the use they make of them. But these and a few others are still not enough for thirteen million people.

So I thought, we ought to watch for our genius colored children and at the expense of all of us, if by no other way, we ought to develop those children and make them feel responsible to their own people so that they will not simply use what has been given them for selfish ends, but for the good of their people. This was no foreign thought to me, for in China this has long been a custom. Any bright boy—I am sorry to say girls were not included until recently—might be chosen by his village for special education and development, with the express purpose of his reflecting honor upon his region and his people. The Chinese have always valued their genius individuals, because they, in common with other peoples of the East believe that a people ought to be guided by their great men. For the same reason they value government officials relatively little. When they are in confusion and trouble they do not look to their government but to their great men for wisdom and spiritual leadership. Thus the people of India have looked and do still look to Gandhi for wisdom.

So it seemed to me that here in my own country a subject people could not look for understanding treatment to a government made up exclusively of persons who belonged to a race which was ridden with prejudice against color. Instead they must look to their own great individuals, and that they might find those great individuals, they must seek them out and help them to grow and not allow them to be lost in the grind of poverty and the lack of opportunity.

To be sure, this would be a slow process. At least a generation would have to pass before there could be results. But there would, I thought, be results sooner or later, not only in leadership for the colored, but in opening the eyes of the blind white people and forcing them to see that a man's color made no difference in his ability to achieve great things.

In the long run of national life the training of all unusually able children would result in the bettering of conditions and even in some measure work against race prejudice, for history shows that two groups tend to approach each other with lessening prejudice as they become more alike in their economic and social standards. Yet to do this it would be necessary to develop colored industry and colored enterprise in all fields, so that colored leaders could find scope.

The second step that I advocated, then, having come thus far, was the building of such enterprise. I remember a speech I once made in New York to a colored audience, in which I endeavored to stir them to some such point of view, urging them to take their money and build opportunity for colored enterprise instead of putting

EQUALITY

their money into such things as Father Divine's heaven. I said, in short, if the white people don't give you a chance in their world, make your own world, and break down race prejudice from your end by taking white employees into your enterprises. I got a good deal of criticism for that speech. My hearers didn't much like it. Father Divine didn't much like it either, and sent somebody to tell me so.

All this was in a sense encouraging. It showed me that the colored people of our country feel they want to be in our nation and not just living here on sufferance. They want to be a part of all American institutions and they have a right to be. The ideal is for colored and white to work together, competing only as individuals and not as groups in our society. But the more I listened and observed and thought, the more impossible it seemed to me that this ideal situation could be realized, at least within a time to be measured in generations and not in centuries. Race prejudice, it seemed to me as I watched it work, could simply checkmate any colored person, unless he had a peculiar individual genius in an art, as a great singer has, or a great chemist. But these in any people are very few indeed, and what of the many who are intelligent and able and yet cannot contribute what they have because they have not a unique genius?

The hard practical question remains, what are we going to do with race prejudice? If we yield to it and build a world within a world, it simply encourages an evil thing. Moreover it deepens the nation's division. Yet if you try to force your way into the white man's world, he resists with the full strength of his prejudice. Moreover, although clamoring at the white man's gate has a nuisance value, yet it is degrading to have to keep clamoring

WHAT AMERICA MEANS TO ME

for that which is your right. It has an effect upon the colored race that is not good. The continued practical state of inferiority, however unjust and undeserved, does affect very much the colored individual and indeed the whole group. Similarly the false assumption of superiority because of race affects just as unfortunately the white man and his group. Race prejudice affects, in short, the whole life of the nation. A lot of people are wasting a lot of time and thought and energy and emotion on something which is sheer nonsense. But there it is. What are we going to do about it?

What are you going to do about it? You can do one of two things—you can accept the situation as it is, you can consider that it will be safest for you to stay inside your own nation, the Negro nation of a white America that will gradually cease to develop in its growth toward true democracy because of its own division. Or you can determine that you are going to help America to be that true democracy of which we dream.

It is more than a dream—it has now become a necessity—that if we are to win the war and to achieve the peace, our country can do so only as a democracy and a united democracy. I tell you frankly that since this war has swept the world into its blaze I have stopped thinking about the rights of the colored people here—I am asking today only one question—how can every citizen in this country fulfil his responsibility as a citizen of our democracy? I repeat, it is as a democracy that we will win this war. If we cease to be a democracy, we will not win this war, and there will not be any peace if we do not win the war.

Therefore it is not enough merely to join the army and the navy and the air forces if they will have us, and

EQUALITY

to do nothing if they will not. It is not enough to pour our savings into war bonds. It is not enough to put our lives into factories and war work so far as we are allowed. We will not win this war unless we win it as a nation where human beings are equal and human rights are respected. The peace will be no peace unless it is based upon the principles of human equality.

In profound belief in democracy, then, in deepest love of our country, let us now realize that when we work for democracy in our own nation we are in the most important sense working for victory in war and in peace.

Discrimination in our country must go, because until it does, we will not have won the war. We cannot fight for freedom unless we fight for freedom for all. We are not better than fascists if we fight for the freedom of one group and not another, for the benefit of one race and not another, for the aggrandizement of a part and not the betterment of the whole. And we must be better than fascists. We cannot allow in our nation the evil root of something which Hitler has developed into a system of slavery the like of which the world has never seen, where the individual is nothing but a piece of property seized and used and tossed aside by a robber government. Japan's militarists, too, have for generations conceived the individual to be nothing but a tool; the history of Japan during the last four generations has been the history of the struggle between the individual and the possessor state. And the beginning of that struggle anywhere is always in the degradation of a class, the condemnation for some trivial cause of a group of individuals.

It is ironic that in Germany the death grip of the state today upon the individual arose not out of too much unity but too little. Germany has never really achieved a sense of nationhood. A loose handful of states, her peoples have longed for unity. But in the desire to be integrated into a nation, they have handed themselves over to a handful of persons who have wrecked them not only as a nation but as individuals.

We, too, are not a unified people. We have sprung from many sources and many places, and we too have a deep seated longing for unity. Perhaps that is why we exalt more than most democracies do the power of our government. In a common government we find a sort of unity which otherwise we lack. Perhaps that is why we look to government instead of to our wise men, as the Chinese and Indians do. But this desire to be unified must not lead us in the direction of the Nazis, where first a race was despised and then every individual who differed from the unifying force was eliminated. The danger in race prejudice always is that it tends to lump people together, and to ignore the individual. Any nation which tolerates prejudice against one group in its people carries inside itself the potentiality of developing fascism, as a persistent sore is always a potential cancer. It has to be watched, and the body is never safe until the sore is cut out.

The equality of opportunity, therefore, which you have not been given in your country has now become more than an individual handicap, more than a group misfortune. It has become a national danger of the sharpest sort, a rock upon which our whole nation may founder. It is now necessary that all of us who believe with all our hearts in democracy work together to bring about human equality in the world of which our nation is only a part.

EQUALITY

There are nations in the world, and great peoples, who may be our friends or our enemies in years soon to come depending upon whether or not we can believe in and practice human equality. I speak of the peoples of Russia and China and India. These three peoples, combined, make most of the world's population. Combined, they hold the future of the world among them. Two of them, China and Russia, are already resolved on the equality of races, and India wants her freedom. They have suffered, two of them, India and China, severely—India disastrously—from the effects of race prejudice. In a world where these nations will have power, and that is already today, they will not tolerate discrimination between peoples. It is essential that these nations be friends with us, and not enemies. But they cannot be wholly our friends if within our own people we are divided by prejudice, one group against another.

You see how important you have become. You are no longer a minority group in one nation. You have become the touch-stone of democracy in our own country, in the world.

For in a sense America has long been the land of dream for many peoples. Many Indians today hoping for freedom look at this moment to our country. Will America really stand for freedom for all? Do the four freedoms apply to an Indian in India? He does not know—but he hopes. And Chinese fighting so bravely and long against the bitter enemy, they look to America. Will America help the Chinese as they are helping the English? And after the war is over, will Americans give to Chinese an equal place, the place they deserve in the world? China does not know.

These are the two countries who have suffered most

heavily from the race prejudice of the white man. And yet why do I not speak of the millions in Java and the South Seas, and in the Philippines and in Africa, and the Arabs? They look to America, who has never wanted an empire, who fought a war for freedom from an empire, and fought another war to free her own slaves—surely America will be on their side?

Yet who dares to promise them that we will be? I dare not. Today it is my greatest shame that when one of these peoples puts the question to me, will America give us real equality of treatment after this war, I can only say I don't know.

And the reason I don't know, that I dare not promise, that I am not sure of the righteousness of my own people in the world, is because of this miserable race prejudice at home which denies equality to a dark skin. I cannot promise that a dark skin in India or in China will have what we have not given our own.

You see how important American democracy has become—democracy, which is not democracy unless it grows out of human equality. You understand that there are millions of people in the world who are losing hope. For if America, the great, the good, treats its dark citizens less kindly than its white, what hope have they? What is left for them to do except to prepare themselves for war and fight for themselves?

Well, one may say, let this be so. The white man has had his day, and now let the colored man have his.

To this I can only answer that freedom and equality are the precious things and that these would still be lost. It does not matter, from the viewpoint of aeons of history, which is uppermost, colored or white. But it matters to the very bottom of life whether or not the trend

EQUALITY

of our hope is toward freedom and equality or away from it. I do not care whether colored or white rules—in a ruler it is only the individual that matters, if there is not to be freedom anyway. Between a kindly colored ruler and an unkind white one, I should choose the kind man for my own life. But whichever it was, it would make no fundamental difference to the world, if there were not to be the freedom of human equality, if ruler and subject were to be the relationship between individuals.

But today we have not reached that point. We are in the midst of a struggle, in the hour of change, when by determined and unwearying action for freedom we can still shape the world toward freedom. We ought so to act that all we do is designed to break down that which denies equality and forbids freedom.

Therefore you are to be congratulated. You have come to your majority at a time in history when more than ever before all effort for freedom can count. You are trained, intelligent and ready to work. You are citizens in a country which still allows free speech and individual effort. But most important of all—and here is your greatest advantage—you belong to a group which more than any in the world knows what race prejudice is, and how even political freedom cannot do away with it, and you know that it must be done away with if democracy is to prevail. The white citizens of this country in their general ignorance cannot realize as clearly as you do how our nation is threatened by our inner division, and what it means to the world if we do not achieve democracy. But you can realize it, you know what it does in your own lives, in your own minds and wills and characters.

You have a peculiar responsibility then, born Americans, trained and taught as you have been, free to live as Americans in a country pledged to freedom and at this moment fighting for freedom in the world.

And you have a great gift within yourselves. As I have come to know colored Americans, I discern in them generally a kind of character which few white people have. It is not a racial distinction, for I do not believe that character has much to do with race. I do believe, however, that it has a great deal to do with circumstances of life. People who have suffered, people who have had to live with an inescapable trouble, with a permanent handicap of some sort, develop either a corroding bitterness or a deep, wise philosophical outlook on life. It is to the great credit of colored Americans that most of them have not grown bitter, but have brought their rich sense of humor and their natural wisdom to bear upon the circumstances which have surrounded them, so that today I say with complete truth that I find more maturity of spirit among the colored people than among any others in this country. I am used to that maturity, for the Chinese, being so wise and old a people, have the same maturity and to a superlative degree. In this regard you are better fitted than any other Americans to establish close relationships with such people as the Chinese and the Indians. Life has taught you something—something which your ancestors had to learn and which they passed on from generation to generation; today you have it as your spiritual possession, and a priceless possession it is—wisdom of the soul.

You are therefore in a superior position in the world today. You are in a superior position in America. It is not you who bear the stigma of not practicing democracy. You have now the advantage over the white man.

EQUALITY

You can be free from hypocrisy. Do not for one moment then accept the status which race prejudice puts upon you. Consider what you can do best and do it, determined never to yield to undemocratic behavior and prejudice which denies all that America means.

You belong here in America—you have a purpose to fulfill in this country. I am grateful that the people of our country are of more races than one. It gives us this matchless opportunity of working out upon our own soil the world problems of equality and of cooperation between different peoples. Do not yield to discouragement or to hopelessness and do not expect an easy life or seek a sheltered one. The times are demanding now that every one of you think not of yourself or of your own race and group life, but of the life of the nation as a whole. All that we have done for democracy in our history will have been lost, if we do not achieve democracy now.

Do not yield then for one moment to anything in our national life which denies democracy. Press steadily for human equality, not only for yourselves but for all those groups who are not given equality. It is as important for you to care that justice is given to a Jew as it is to fight for it for yourself. It is the principle that must be established for all of us, or none of us will have it.

You will ask me, how can this be done?

Well, the spirit in which it is done is the first thing. I should like to see colored Americans show their belief in human equality as a principle by making it apply to others beyond themselves. The fight against discrimination in this country, for example, would have added force if the colored people would show some interest in the way other people, also colored, are being treated. I should like to have colored opinion express itself clearly on the matter, for example, of Chinese immigration into this country. China is our great and brave ally—we are her ally, rather, for it is she who has fought the war thus far, and we have done very little even to aid her. I should like to see colored Americans take a leading part in modifying, for example, our very discriminatory immigration laws which forbid a quota to Chinese immigration. Now of all times would be the time, when China is so sorely pressed by our common enemy, for America to come forward with an act which proves to Chinese that we are determined to give up race prejudice as a motive for our actions.

I should like to see colored Americans press for more aid to China in planes and war materials. We have given China a few old fashioned planes from which we even removed the radios at the last moment. We are talking of sending a few more. That is all we have done. Yet China is trying to go on trusting us as an ally. It is not easy. It is less easy, I can tell you, when she observes the segregation in our army and navy and air forces. It is inevitable that she concludes that America will help the white people with all our force, as we are now helping England, but that America will not help China because she is not white. I cannot deny, when I am pressed by Chinese questions, that this is true, at least in its practical effect, and I say it with anger and sorrow. I should like to be able to tell my Chinese friends that Americans are not like that. But I cannot.

And I should like you to take a deep interest in India, who has been so unjustly treated in our press and by our radio commentators and columnists. With what childish arrogance these men in their ignorance of history and

EQUALITY

their complete ignorance of India have dared to criticize and to judge India at this time when after years of patient effort, she has again been denied freedom. You ought to know of India, and for our country's sake you ought to let India know that there are Americans who understand her point of view and who sympathize with her desire for freedom and her wish to work out her own problems of national unity.

And what do you know of Korea, that people long subject to the military rule of Japan and now longing for *their* freedom, and what of the people of Indonesia? For America's sake, you must mend the ignorance of the white American and atone for his arrogance, and do what he has not been willing to do for these who look to America to lead in democracy.

If I have a criticism to make of the colored people of our country it is that they have been too selfish in their interest in equality. They have thought too often of equality only for themselves in this one country—and by so doing they have limited their own struggle and robbed it of size and force and meaning for the whole human race. You are not simply a group of people in one country—you are part of the great war of the peoples for freedom. They are not only colored peoples against white—there are many white people on your side, and white people in many parts of the world who are subject, too, to tyrants. You must understand the meaning of the war, and you must wage it on its true scale. By linking your particular battle for your own place in your own country to the whole war for freedom and human equality in the world, you will enlarge your forces and strengthen your cause, and help to win the war for democracy.

WHAT AMERICA MEANS TO ME

And you must remember that if we are really to achieve human equality in the world the war must not degenerate into a war of the races or a war of East against West. Such a struggle between prejudices will win nothing. Your enemies are not of one race or nation, your enemies are all those who do not believe in human equality, who judge a man by his skin and not by what he is as an individual. Your allies are those who believe in and practice human equality and who judge an individual solely by what he is and what he does. As simply as that, you may know your enemies from your allies. You too must not yield to race prejudice. It is as wrong for you to hate the white man because he is white as it is for him to hate you because you are not white. Keep yourselves free from jealousy and revenge that you may do your great work in the world in this time.

And what is your work? It is to be a bridge between your country and those other countries of which I have just spoken. The white man perhaps cannot understand India as India now needs to be understood, nor will he help China as China ought now to be helped. But you can understand India, because you know what India has had to suffer, and you know what China needs now and at the peace table.

Come out of that little world of your own and take your place in America as interpreters of the colored peoples of the world. Be ready to speak for Africa at the peace table, and to speak for Korea. Make yourselves the part of America to whom these peoples turn for understanding. Today you belong to the world, and your demands in your own country are part of the world demand for freedom and for human equality.

You must, in short, stop thinking of yourselves as col-

EQUALITY

ored people in a white country. You must instead think of yourselves as people determined with other people to make democracy come true. Forget the color of your skins. How can you ask white people to forget your color if you cannot forget it? When you really believe that it makes no difference what color your skin is, you can step out of yourselves, free. You must, in your own spirit, be equal to any other people before you are equal. Be free, and you can act as free people. Be equal, and you will act as human beings equal to any and all. Drive out of yourselves first the very memory of any difference between peoples—deny it by what you are. Go to your great work in the world of today unhampered by the thought of race prejudice in others or in yourselves.

As far as you are able really to believe in your own equality, so far will you be able to bring about human equality in our country and in the world. You will not grow bigger than your own feelings, you will not accomplish more than you are. This fight for equality begins in your own soul, and then it must spread as wide as the world. The battle against race prejudice is no longer a family quarrel in our own house. The great storm that now sweeps humanity has swept us all with it, and our little fight against discrimination has become part of the tremendous struggle for human freedom upon this globe.

Let us enlarge our own minds, then, let us increase the space in our souls, that we may be fit to live through these heroic times.

4. FREEDOM

A VAST dim shape of peoples is now beginning to appear out of this war. It is so dim that it will not be seen by all, and the last people to see it, inevitably, will be those who are in the thick of the active waging of the war, the men who are commanding the battle, at home and abroad. These are the necessary "men of action," whose minds are too busy with the day's work to see beyond it. They are essential men, we cannot do without them, and yet we must not allow all our vision to be bound by the limitations of "men of action."

For the vast dim shape is there. It is not a ghost—it is the first appearance of a reality. And the reality is the world of tomorrow, beginning to take shape out of the world of today. It is not prophecy, it is not guess, it is what is already beginning to happen.

What is this shape? It is the shape of a world in which there is already a new East. The war began in the East, not in Europe, and the primary war is being fought in the East. When peace is made, whether it is made in our time or after it, it will be made in the East.

In the East, the war began in that part which is Japan. The seizure of Manchuria in 1931 was not the beginning of the war, though some have called it that. The

An article published in *Common Sense*, September, 1942.

war was begun in Japan long before that, and it was a civil war. There were no military battles, unless one wishes to call the assassination of liberal ministers of state a battle. The war was between old Japan and new Japan —old Japan, which is the old East of which ancient Japan was a part, and new Japan, which is the West. For Japan, though she became a power in so spectacularly short a time, did not become westernized. Her modernization, so far as it went, was simply the modernization of weapons of war, of ships, of techniques, in industries and education. Japan has not deserved the common accusation of being a "copycat of the West." Never has there been a more independent resistant people than the Japanese. Everything brought in from the West by new Japan was at tremendous cost of struggle against it. It was only with reluctance and out of the bitter necessity of coping with the West that Japan modernized herself at all. In the process there were inevitably individuals who were influenced by Western thinking and civilization. Against these the old Japan fought with ferocity—and now has won. It is old Japan that wages war against the West today, old Japan though fighting with bombers and warships. Her civil war is finished. Her people are unified for the duration. Old Japan has triumphed and is on the offensive against the West.

This triumph of the ancient East has had its inevitable effect upon other countries of Asia. The Pan-Asia of which Japan is dreaming will not come about under her rule, but it may come about. It is the clearest part of tomorrow's vast dim shape. The military triumph of Japan against the West has made Pan-Asia something more than a dream. China, fighting beside the West against Japan, nevertheless has not lost as the white man lost in Burma, in Malaya, in the Netherlands East Indies, and even in the Philippines. For in those losses the East triumphed over the West, and China is part of the East. China was fighting a local war against Japan, but she was also in a larger war, and though she lost the smaller war she gained in the larger one. In so far as Japanese victory has pushed the West out of the East, it has been China's victory, too.

And it has been India's victory. When Japan drove the white man out of his empire in other places she loosened his hold upon India. The slackening of the imperial grasp is felt by millions of hearts hungry for freedom. It explains, more than anything else, what is happening at this moment in India, and what will happen tomorrow.

Something new is coming out of the East. What it is cannot yet be discerned, but it will bring a great change to the whole world. And the reason it cannot yet be clearly discerned is because the shape is not definite. What it will be depends upon the way the West goes. It depends upon the sort of mind that will take power in the West and mold the thoughts of western peoples. There is yet time to make that dim Eastern shape a benevolent one. But unless belated wisdom guides the West, the East will not be benevolent and there may be greater catastrophe than we have yet had. There may be new war with new foes and strange new alliances.

For the triumph of old Japan has awakened the soul of the East, numbed and bewildered with its century-and-a-half of contact with the West. That old East, the spirit of the millions of its people, has wondered at the West, has admired the brilliance of its science, has been

FREEDOM

amused with its mechanical toys, has been terrified, too, by its weapons and terror. But admiration and amusement have passed now. The East has recovered itself, it has decided to revive its own life, to live as it wishes to live. The East has discovered that it can be free.

It is this discovery of the possibility of freedom by those who have not been free which is the most potent force in our world today. Great good may come out of it and great evil. For freedom is man's dream wherever man is found. The ignorant worker on a rubber plantation in Sumatra dreamed of freedom, slave that he was. The Indian in a village, never having seen an Englishman, has known he was not free, and he is hungry and thirsty for freedom, and he will have freedom though he die for it. For this war is larger than the struggle between any two or three nations, larger than our war with Hitler, larger than Japan's war of aggression, larger even than any war for national survival. It is the war for human freedom.

The waiting East, the quiescent, subject East, has seen the possibility of life again, because it can be free. It is with this East that we must live tomorrow, and we had better begin to live with it today. Whatever we fight for, the East fights for freedom, and its peoples will not stop short of freedom, wherever the war leads.

How shall the West be made to understand what is going on in the East? It is our gravest danger that we cannot and even will not understand. We resist the knowledge of the truth. Yet all our defeats thus far have come because of our ignorance and not through lack of integrity or good will, and certainly not through our lack of courage. We peoples of the West are brave people and on the whole honest people. But too many of us are merely men of action, and as men of action we see little and comprehend less of those things which cannot be handled or photographed or put into reports. We scorn the importance of the intangible. Thus France fell, and thus fell the great empires of the West in the East.

What we must see is that this war is not merely the active war now being fought in Europe and the Pacific. These are only the immediate thrusts of war, the parts of the whole upon which the spotlight is being fixed. But the war scene is far greater than the spotlight and it is the whole which must be grasped and understood, for victory only in the military incidents of war will not give us victory in the great war looming around and above and beyond the spotlight. The struggle is not contained in the spotlight.

Where is the struggle? The struggle is in the awakening peoples, all those peoples of the world, who sitting long in darkness, now rise to their feet at the sudden call of that word freedom. In India last spring Madame Chiang Kai-shek, addressing a group of Indian women, besought them to rouse their nation to the danger of the Japanese, and, to make her plea strike to their hearts as it came from her own, she told them with fearful realism of the tortures which the women and children of China have suffered at the hands of the enemy. There was sympathy, there was sorrow, but at the end of the meeting an Indian woman got up and her voice rang over the room. "Let no one imagine," she said clearly, "that it can make any possible difference to us whether it is the Japanese or the British who rule India."

An Englishman, a man of goodwill and integrity, hearing this was amazed, "Curiously irrelevant," he exclaimed, in telling of the incident, "in grating discord with the prevailing mood!"

He did not see the larger war and he could not understand the vastness of the dim shape looming. No, not irrelevant, and not in discord with that. There comes a moment to human beings, after long endurance, when nothing is worth having if it is not freedom and nothing is more hateful than the lack of it. Then all the practical benefits of benevolent rule seem no better than the evils of tyranny because there is not freedom. Can we who are white and free ever understand this? Perhaps not, for we have always possessed freedom, that natural right of man, and we have possessed it so long that many of us have forgotten that it is a natural right. And yet we in America ought not to make this mistake. "We hold these truths to be self-evident, that all men are created equal, that they are endowed by their Creator with certain unalienable Rights, that among these are Life, Liberty and the Pursuit of Happiness. That to secure these Rights, Governments are instituted among Men, deriving their just powers from the consent of the governed."

It was an Englishman, Henry W. Nevinson, who said, "You know what freedom is when you have not got it." He was right—none who have always been free can understand the terrible fascinating power of the hope of freedom to those who are not free. But we must understand, we free peoples of the West, if we are to understand what is happening today in the East and why it is happening. We must not be controlled by those who are not able to understand.

The governor of Alabama, protesting against a federal contract which calls for no discrimination in labor on the grounds of color or creed, says "The State of Alabama is not willing to enter into any contract in which this clause appears. . . . I regard it as extremely unfortunate that this issue should be forced upon the southern people in a time when the very life of the nation is at stake. . . . There should be no attack on the long-established institutions of any section when our sons are engaged in a life and death struggle with the enemies of the democratic way of life. . . . The Democratic Party in Alabama has as its motto, 'White Supremacy.' " *

But the peoples who are waging the large war cry out in answer, "How can democracy and white supremacy be spoken of in the same breath? For what do your sons die when they die for democracy, if it is not for democracy for all?"

The Secretary of State, Cordell Hull, in his address to the American people of July 23, 1942, said, "It has been our purpose in the past—and will remain our purpose in the future—to use the full measure of our influence to support attainment of freedom by all peoples who, by their acts, show themselves worthy of it and are ready for it."

And the peoples who are not free cry, "Who made you who are white the judges to decide who are worthy of freedom, who are ready for freedom? Is freedom something to be attained, or is it man's natural right? Have you not said yourselves that man is born free?"

In spite of any efforts to limit it, this war is becoming a war for human freedom everywhere, and that is the greatest war that can be waged by humankind. The issue with Japan may be lost in it, and so may the issue with Germany. Our limited war aims of maintaining

* *Congressional Record,* Page A-3165, July 24, 1942.

FREEDOM

our standards of living, of preserving our sectional prejudices, of keeping the seas open, of maintaining our centers of power in the Orient, of getting back to the "status quo"—however we cling to these hopes of a limited war they are being swept from us. Peoples are taking this war out of the hands of governments and militarists. They are sweeping away the men of small minds.

What then shall we do? We may, if we like, do nothing, except to deny the truth. It is always possible to deny the intangible, to refuse its inevitability, to cling to the limits of what is plain to the limited vision. In that case the vast dim shape beyond the spotlight will loom larger and blacker. For when we in America will admit no change in our way of thinking and in our way of life, it means among other things that white Americans in the South will go on insisting on no change in the status of the colored Americans. If we are pressed too hard by the yeast of freedom, we can put it down by force. And England can go on insisting that India is not to have freedom now, and England can go on trying to put down by force India's rebellion.

But while we do these things we are taking great risk of losing the real war. For as we fail to suppress freedom —and inevitably we must fail—we will grow afraid and our fear will open the door to Hitler and to others like him. These will say, and to ready listeners, since prejudice is often stronger than patriotism, "Let all white peoples join together. We must stick together, we white peoples."

On the day when the white peoples agree to join together against the rest of the world the shape in the East will spring clearly into the sight of all. We shall see it, the blindest and the most stupid of us. And Russia will be with the East, not the West, whether vanquished or victorious over Hitler now. Pan Asia will not be a dream on that day. It will be a reality but it will not be Japan's Pan Asia. It will be Pan Asia, more than one-half of the world. You can see the shape, now.

If we go on as we are, taking cognizance only of the things which are happening on the battlefields, if we refuse to hear that great tocsin for Freedom that echoes in all the peoples who are not free, the day will come—it takes no prophet to declare it—when we shall have to fight for our own freedom against most fearful odds of revenge and bitterness—revenge for what is now history, and bitterness because in these days when we could all yet be saved, we do nothing.

For it is possible to do something. It is possible first to recognize the size of this war, to understand the power of the word Freedom and to use it. We hang back, we are afraid to speak out boldly and tell these hungering and thirsting peoples that they shall have freedom and have it now.

"It was much, no doubt," an Englishman associated with the Cripps Mission to India says, "to ask that, having waited so long to acquire the right to determine their national destiny, the Congress leaders should wait a little longer; but now that its acquisition was assured them immediately after the war, provided only that the United Nations won it, and in view of the practical necessities of the present situation, was it too much to ask?"

We must understand that it was too much to ask of people who had fought bravely through the first world war, being under the impression, whether rightly or

FREEDOM

wrongly, given them consciously or unconsciously, that they would have the right to determine their national destiny afterward. Twenty-three years have passed, a generation in India, and they have not been given the right to determine their national destiny, the right, that is, with which every man is born. After a hundred and fifty years, and a promise, and then twenty-three years of waiting for the promise, and then another promise— whatever the western point of view, to the man in the East it was too long to wait. To do nothing, therefore, in the view of this world longing for freedom, does this mean that we are afraid of freedom for the peoples not our own, the races not our own? Do we fear a free Indian, and a free colored man in America? The uneasy memory of what is past is in us. Revenge is human.

What we must now realize is that there is a chance for us to wipe out that past by present action. Swift and clear action now for freedom for all will make amends for the denials of freedom in the past. But it must be action and not promises of "after the war." Even our friends and allies the Chinese are cynical about those promises. The truth is, we have carried promises to the limits of absurdity. Let us make no more—let us act to make good our true intention. Only thus can revenge be forgotten.

But when we have acted, when we have set free, so far as is in our power, the peoples of the East, need we be afraid? The white race is in the minority in the world. Need we fear the colored peoples? I am perhaps the last person to answer the question for I cannot understand such fear. I have lived almost all my life, sometimes entirely solitary in great communities of non-white peoples, all the time nearly solitary, and I have seen nothing to fear among those peoples. They are more amiable, more laughter-loving, more kindly in personal ways, than the white peoples are. Their minds are not filled with constant thoughts of conquest. We say continually to ourselves as I heard an American say the other day that "somebody must be top dog, and we had better be it." But the man of the East, who has his own faults and cruelties, is not continually thinking in terms of conquest and top dog. If he is not more benevolent than we are, at least he is equally so.

Our benevolence is of differing kinds. I will give an example. The man of the West is benevolent when he makes laws for the insane which put the crippled mind or body into institutions segregated from the community. The man in the East considers it cruel to separate the afflicted from those most likely to give him real affection and care, his family. And again, if children are better protected from oppressive labor in the West, old people are treated far more humanely in the East. You may take your choice of benevolence, East and West, but there is no need to be afraid. There is no choice between colors for cruelty, either. East and West, Germans and Japanese, have run a neck-and-neck race in cruelty in this war.

We need these days to give up our absurd fears of the Oriental. Occidental is as fearsome a word in the East and yet they are only two words, and colors are only colors. Human beings in the East proportionately are as good and as just, as human beings are in the West. If they have not organized justice in the way that we have in our modern forms, their hearts and practices are the same. I see no better men here in my own country than I saw in China or India—and no worse.

FREEDOM

And it is to be remembered that out of the East have come our deepest religions and philosophies. Christ was an Oriental, even as Confucius was, and Buddha, and it was in the Near East that the springs for the Renaissance in Europe were found. It may be in the East again that we will find once more those springs, if today we can take advantage of our great opportunity to convince the peoples there of our sincerity in wanting them to have freedom, freedom from domination by our race, by our empires. If when our domination is withdrawn they fall into subjection to others, that is not our fault, and they must struggle free of those, too, and we ought to help in that struggle, if we believe in freedom.

Nothing but good to us will come out of an East that is free. Ruler and subject, governor and governed, must not be the human relations between East and West. Co-operation can be the relation, if we are willing to make it so. And we ought to give the great civilizations of the East their chance now, for they are based upon the primary importance of human relationships, a notion strange to us, but which for all that may hold the key to the future. Our own record for the last three centuries in the West is damning enough.

The simple necessity today is to accept the fact that the real war is about freedom, and to declare that freedom is a natural right and that the peoples shall be free. And what is freedom? Simply that all shall be considered equal as human beings; that there is to be no further subjection of peoples by peoples or races by races. That is what the East means by freedom. The West must mean it, too.

So simple a statement, so straightforward an action, would swing the millions of the East, yes, and those still not free in the West, to our side. Then Hitler could not win by guile and Japan could not win by arms. The peoples longing for freedom would swarm to our standard, if we made that standard Freedom. And that vast dim shape of Tomorrow—we would not need to fear it any more.

But of course we would have to mean what we said. That is, we must, first, really want all peoples to be free.

5. THE MEANING OF INDIA

I RECEIVED not long ago an interesting letter from a man at Yale University. He will not mind, I am sure, if I quote from it here. He wrote:

Many Yale alumni have asked me, "Why are Yale undergraduates and recent graduates so indifferent over what is going on in Europe?" My answer has been that they are not indifferent; that they are merely baffled by the discrepancy between the President's idealistic statements and the indifference to the wretched status of the Negro in this country and of the hundreds of millions of subjects of the British Empire in India, of so many supporters of his foreign policy. I pointed out that, during the last ten or fifteen years, Yale, along with every other good American university, has offered excellently taught and widely attended courses in sociology and in the history of European imperialism. These have given the students facts which university students of my day were not taught in college and did not, with few exceptions, learn afterwards. I believe and said that the Yale undergraduate would continue to regard his participation in the war as an unpleasant necessity and not as a matter for enthusiasm until the idealists who have supported our position in the war have the sense and the courage to demand the same treatment for the Negro in

A speech at a meeting for the India League of America, in Town Hall, New York, September 30, 1942.

WHAT AMERICA MEANS TO ME

America and the Indian in India as we are fighting for in the case of the German Jew, the Pole, or the Norwegian in Europe.

It is not only undergraduates and recent graduates of Yale University who are baffled today by the discrepancy between idealistic statements about this war and indifference to the actual carrying out of those statements.

There are some persons, of course, who cry out against idealism. Idealism, they say, is always getting us into trouble. This is quite true. People on the whole are very simple-minded, in whatever country one finds them. They are so simple as to take literally, more often than not, the things their leaders tell them. The four freedoms rang over the world like the call of a bugle.

"Freedom of speech—everywhere in the world.

"Freedom of every person to worship God in his own way—everywhere in the world.

"Freedom from want—everywhere in the world.

"Freedom from fear—everywhere in the world."

The four freedoms were explained thus by the President:

"These Freedoms are separate but not independent. Each one relies upon all the others. Each supports the whole, which is liberty. When one is missing all the others are jeopardized. A person who lives under a tyrant and has lost freedom of speech must necessarily be tortured by fear. A person who is in great want is usually also in great fear—fear of even direr want and greater insecurity. A person denied the right to worship in his own way has thereby lost the knack of free speech, for unless he is free to exercise his religious conscience, his privilege of free speech (even though not specifically

THE MEANING OF INDIA

denied) is meaningless. A person tortured with fears has lost both the privilege and the strength to supply himself with his needs." And a little further on there is this sentence. "To be free a man must live in a society which has relieved those curious pressures which conspire to make men slaves; pressure of a despotic government, pressure of intolerance, pressure of want."

Brave good words! It is no wonder that everywhere the hearts of the people stirred, the hearts of the dark people, the hearts of the light people. These are fine fighting words. Men and women will give up all they have if they can hope to make a world where they and their children shall live free.

What was the matter, I wonder? What made the gold come off these words? Perhaps the Atlantic Charter did the first damage. When India was excepted from this free world, there was a slight cloud, not bigger than a man's hand, upon the four freedoms in which we all believed, for which we were all willing to give our lives. Then, of course, it was true, that some of us drew hasty conclusions. The Negroes here in our country were actually taking seriously these four freedoms. It was often embarrassing. Churchill, honest man, blurted out exactly what was in his mind—that of course the Atlantic Charter did not apply to India! I admire his honesty with all my heart. We could not be quite so honest. We tried to put the whole matter aside, or some of us did, by saying that what we are fighting for is much more realistic than the four freedoms. Brave words are necessary to rouse the public, but only realists know what the war is about. It is a war to defeat Germany and Japan. But somehow that truth has not been enough to make our people go into this war with enthusiasm. If freedom is only for part of the world and for some peoples, instead of, as the four freedoms had led us to think, being something for humanity, there is always the fear that those who are deprived may turn some day. That is, unless all are free, none can be free from fear of the loss of freedom.

Now the professional realist will always say that such general aims are the dreams of idealists—a war to end war, for instance, and freedom for all, and human equality. These are utopias, and we had better forget them and get down to business. "Let's mobilize all our efforts to fight this war."

This sounds wonderful. We are all eager to get down to fighting and winning this war. A great victory at this moment would be the most welcome news this side of heaven. If realism can win it, three cheers for realism. But if we are going in for facts, we must also face the fact that we are not mobilizing all our efforts. People who are baffled can't mobilize all their efforts. Our people are baffled. The people of India and China are baffled. Obviously the people of England are baffled. I do not doubt that the waiting people of France and Poland and Norway are baffled. We have had proof in the last week or two of the complete and angry bafflement of the people of Russia.

It is this bafflement which is robbing our war effort of half its strength. People who go to war as a matter of unpleasant necessity and not with enthusiasm are not in a winning mood. They are not even in a good fighting mood. We are baffled by the discrepancy between declaration and action, and India is one of the chief examples of this discrepancy.

I do not consider the independence of India, or of

THE MEANING OF INDIA

any one country, at this hour, as a cause important enough in itself to spend time and thought upon if it were a matter apart from the successful waging of this war. Were there no war, I would even say that the independence of India was a business chiefly England's and India's. I would say that India must struggle for her freedom exactly as we had to do. Of course I believe that freedom is a human right. If one stands by the Declaration of Independence it is un-American and undemocratic to say that anybody must "achieve" freedom or "deserve" freedom or any such nonsense. The only kind of a world fit for human beings is a world where everybody is born free. Yet people have often to fight to assert that right, and so India, had there been no world war, would have had to assert her rights for herself. I would not have felt it necessary, except through motives of altruism or abstract idealism, that we, for instance, should go to her aid. France once came to our aid in like circumstances, it is true, and in every nation you will find men like Byron, of England, who for sheer adoration of human freedom, went to Greece and died for it.

But it is in no such mood of altruism or idealism that we must now give heed to India. We must now think about India for the simplest of reasons, one which even the realists honor, that of self-interest. It is to our interest today, in this war still undecided, that we summon every possible ally to our one aim of *victory*—not only allies who are people, but allies of the mind, faith in our cause, and belief that our victory is victory for the right. How else can we take away this bafflement that dims faith and makes victory seem so far away? It is not enemy propaganda which does the damage. Nor must we heed that hush-hush cry, that refuge of all who do not want truth revealed, who say whenever we face our own souls, "You are helping Hitler!" They will lose this war for us if we heed them. For we must have faith in what we do before we can do it, and faith comes only when we are not afraid to know the truth.

Let us consider the truth as it is now known about India. In the first place let us face the fact of our ignorance of India. The people of India have always been remote from us. Most of us have never seen their faces. We know nothing of the language of the people of India. We have few sources of knowledge about India. Even the English who have ruled India have known the people very little. Least of all have those known India who have governed her people directly, although they have lived their lives out under Indian skies and upon Indian soil and the bread they have eaten has been paid for out of taxes upon the Indian people. On the whole they have not been bad men. But they have lived within their walls of prestige—imperial and racial prestige. There is no real communication possible between people who rule and the ones whom they rule.

Here in America, in our usual kindly thoughtlessness, we have never considered India in our world or any of our business. The thoughtless and the ignorant still contend that India is none of our business. Yet I believe that India is a matter of life and death to us.

We know Gandhi a little, of course—that incomprehensible man, launching his civil disobedience movement when it is so sorely inconvenient! We might understand him better if we knew where he got the idea of civil disobedience. It was partly, at least, from a good

THE MEANING OF INDIA

American, a Yankee, Henry David Thoreau. It began about 1893, and Gandhi was a young lawyer in South Africa, trying to help the plight of his fellow Indians there who were laborers under practically slave conditions. Then he chanced one day to find that essay of Thoreau's entitled "Civil Disobedience." You will remember it—Thoreau had refused to pay his poll tax. He didn't believe in the poll tax, and besides, the proceeds of the tax were being used to finance the Mexican war in which he did not believe either. So he was sent to jail. In jail he wrote:

I have paid no poll tax for six years. I was put into jail on this account and as I stood considering the walls of solid stone two or three feet thick, the door of wood and iron, a foot thick, and the iron grating which strained the light, I could not help being struck with the foolishness of the institution which treated me as if I were mere flesh and blood and bones to be locked up. I wondered that it should have concluded at length that this was the best use it could put me to, and had never thought to avail itself of my services in some other ways!

In jail Jawaharlal Nehru—one of the few men who today might convince the people of India that this is their war because it is a war for freedom for them as for the people of Poland and Norway and France—Nehru writes:

The years I have spent in prison, sitting alone, wrapped in my own thoughts! How many seasons have I seen go by, following one another into oblivion! How many moons have I watched wax and wane and the pageant of the stars moving along, inexorably and majestically! How many yesterdays of my youth lie buried here! Sometimes I see the ghosts of the dead yesterdays rise up, bringing poignant memories. They stand whispering to me, was it worth while?

And then he too finds comfort in Thoreau and quotes this from him:

Under a government which imprisons any unjustly, the true place for a just man is in prison.

I hold no brief for civil disobedience, you may be sure. But the fact of Gandhi's reliance on Thoreau might help Americans to understand India better at this moment, when for our own sakes we had better understand India.

When this war broke out we were still so ignorant that we really never thought of India as in our world. We did not think of India much until Hong Kong fell and Singapore fell and Malaya fell and Burma fell. India was next and we began suddenly to feel we ought to know something about India. Besides, American men were going over there.

But it was inexplicably hard to find out anything about India. We may as well face the fact of censorship. Censorship is necessary in a war. It was about this time that I carried on a lively but private correspondence with one of our leading newspapers. I felt we must learn something about India, and yet in spite of the most careful study of that newspaper I could learn nothing that could be called impartial. All the news came through non-Indian sources. When I wrote to the editor asking why this was so, I discovered that they had no Indian sources of news. I am glad to say that this situation has now been changed.

The Indian people suffer the same difficulty about us. They know as little about us as we about them. They

THE MEANING OF INDIA

want to know what we think and feel about them. What they are given is every intemperate, hasty, prejudiced hostile, ignorant word we have said. It is no wonder that deep distrust of America is beginning to darken Indian hearts. So far as they are allowed to know we disapprove them completely. So far as they know, we are standing for empire.

We might say that it is not important to us what India thinks of us or whether she knows us or not. Legally she is part of Britain's Empire and Britain is our ally. Let us stick to our facts. India is a continent of 390,000,000 people, about three times as many people as we have, and about ten times as many as England has. Speaking merely from the point of view of the realists, that is, from the point of view of self-interest, it would be an advantage to us if we could interest these millions or even a part of them in this war. There are a million or more of them already in the Indian army. We must face the fact that at least some of these are poor men who entered the army in order to have food and clothing and shelter.

It is a fact, and one which I have seen with my own eyes more than once, that India is the poorest country in the Orient. I had always thought the Chinese were rather poor, until I went to India. The difference between the two countries is appalling. The people of India are infinitely poorer than the people of China. There are of course many reasons for this. Let me refer you to that excellent book by Kate Mitchell, entitled *India Without Fable*. You will find the reasons for India's poverty clearly explained there. I wish merely to state the fact, which everyone knows who has been to India, that the people there are very poor indeed, and

WHAT AMERICA MEANS TO ME

we must naturally realize that some of them do enter the army as mercenaries. Even so, an army of even two million is too small an army from a continent of 390,000,000. We must conclude, therefore, that under the present reign of realism, the people of India are not being mobilized adequately from a military point of view.

But what of the people? Perhaps if Japan invades India the people will resist whether they are mobilized or not. They will undoubtedly. They will resist as well as they can. Those who know them best testify to that. And there is no doubt when one talks with Indians, even the Indian Nationalists, that although they want to be free to work out their own problems of government, yet if they cannot be free they prefer the empire they know to one they do not know. They have no illusions about Japan. They know what Japan has done in China and elsewhere. But let Nehru himself speak for these Nationalists. He says:

"We are not going to embarrass Britain's war effort in India or those of our American friends who may come here. I want to fight this idea that we must remain passive and cannot do anything against the Japanese invasion."

And again, in an interview a few days before his arrest he said that India would be a partner of the United Nations and would never make a separate peace with Japan. He added, "India of course is anxious to see the complete freedom of all Asiatic countries. War cannot be carried on unless it is a people's war."

And as far back as May 5, 1942, the working Committee of the India Congress Party voted, as follows: "In case invasion takes place it must be resisted. Such

THE MEANING OF INDIA

resistance can only take the form of non-violent non-cooperation, as the British Government prevented organization of national Defenses by the people in any other way. We may not bend the knee to the aggressor nor obey any of his orders. We may not look to him for favors, nor fall to his bribes. If he wishes to take possession of our homes and our fields, we must refuse to give them up, even if we have to die in the effort to resist him."

There is much evidence in many places that the people of India will not welcome Japan and that they will resist by every means in their power.

Unfortunately those means are weak and few. Almost the only resistance they can make, if and when Japan comes in, is the ineffectual one of non-cooperation. It is not that they want no other means. They long for weapons. But weapons have never been allowed to the people of India. It is against the law for them to have even a knife more than a few inches long, and concealed weapons constitute a crime there as here, India has no arms. It will not be possible therefore, for India to come to her own defense. We allied nations must somehow send enough armed men to India, to hold India.

Let us ask a realistic question. If we send the huge armies necessary, the vast supplies, what guarantee have we that the people would cooperate with us? Perhaps like the people of Burma and Malaya they will turn and help the enemy against us. How do the people of India feel toward us?

Just at this point, and only for a moment, let me divide "us" into England and America. England's is the responsibility for India, but American men are now being asked to defend India as part of the allied strategy.

WHAT AMERICA MEANS TO ME

We may therefore ask what is India's attitude toward us who are Americans?

To put it in a phrase, I may say she is still hopeful. She remembers the name George Washington. She still thinks it is possible that we may understand her wish to be assured of freedom after the war. I don't think any Indians expect freedom now. They are a very reasonable people. Like the Chinese they have had so long a human history that they take into account men's motives, and the situation of nations. They understand how dependent upon India has been the British Empire. What they ask is assurance for the future. They would like assurance from us of our sympathy with their longing to be free. They would like assurance from England that they will be free after this war.

But, you will say, that assurance has been given. Let us face the facts—it has *not* been given. You will say it was given by the Cripps Mission. The fact is that in the form to which Sir Stafford Cripps was forced to reduce his original offer to the Indians, independence was not assured.

You may say, and perhaps rightly, that even so the leaders of India ought to have mobilized in so far as they were able, their own people. But it is probable that the Indians feared that a retreat would leave great regions of India open to the enemy. If people are to fight for themselves they must have leaders in whom they have absolute confidence and they must have arms. It was upon this matter of the defense of a defenseless people that the leaders of India felt they had to make a stand. This required that Indian leaders in charge of defense be given the final decision on matters regarding defense.

THE MEANING OF INDIA

The lives of India's people were dependent upon this. You can see what a tremendous responsibility faced the leaders of the Indian people. They were willing to take it to save India. We ought to admire their splendid courage in a desperate situation. And yet even they knew that the task was impossible if they were not given the power to do it.

Were the effects of these facts confined only to India we might still accept them. But the further fact is that we could make India the arsenal of the East. The resources of India are enormous, if we could use them, if we could mobilize quickly enough the industries necessary to develop them. In spite of the abject poverty of India's people, India herself is fabulously rich. Her natural resources rival our own or the Soviet Union's. She has one of the largest iron ore fields in the world, with reserves of three billion tons averaging a 64 per cent iron content. Indian coal reserves are estimated at 36 billion to 60 billion tons. She has huge supplies of manganese and 49 per cent of the world's bauxite. She has great deposits of chromite, mica, copper ore, and other valuable minerals. Her potential hydro-electric power resources are second only to our own. She is one of the world's leading agricultural nations in spite of the fact that her methods are still primitive. Her output of wheat, rice, cotton, jute, silk, oil, seeds, hemp, tobacco, sugar and other commodities entitle her to rank as one of the leaders in these products. She is the world's second largest cotton producer. She is first in jute. In 1936-37 she was first in tobacco. In 1939-1940 she was first in sugar production. She is the world's leading producer of hides and skins, while her endless forests provide a limitless supply of tanning materials, as well as timber, lac, turpentine, and bamboo pulp.*

India has a vast labor supply of skilled craftsmen trained through the ages in beautiful fine crafts, men now starving on the farms to which they have had to return because of the lack of industrial development of the country. India's population has not increased at the rate that it is commonly reported. In fact, the rate of increase has been lower than any country of Europe in the same periods. Between 1880 and 1930 the population of England and Wales increased by 54 per cent, and India by only 32 per cent. Only in 1920-1931 was the increase in India higher than in England, and even so it was much lower than ours, 10.6 per cent as compared to our own 14.2.

India desperately needs industries, and her people would welcome them. Why not, when the great majority of Indian people live on incomes of from two to four cents a day? Do not think that they live well according to Oriental standards. I have seen what they eat and how they live. They eat and live miserably and they know it.

Under our present policy we are just writing India off. But unfortunately it is not only a question of India —it is a question of China also. If we write India off we must write China off, too, and for this reason: if we lose India, China will be entirely isolated. We can neither get help to her nor from her. Those beautiful air bases which thousands of Chinese are at this moment fighting and dying to gain and to hold against that day when we shall really bomb Japan will be lost to us then. I am asked very often these days, "In case China is isolated will she

* See *India Without Fable,* by Kate L. Mitchell.

THE MEANING OF INDIA

give up to Japan?" I say no, but she will have to fight a different sort of war from the one she is fighting today. It would be folly for her to fight as she is doing now, surrounded on four sides by the enemy and beyond hope of any aid. She will have to return to her ancient ways, the ways in which she has conquered all others who have conquered her. She will be lost to us, for the time being at least. We must reckon with that. It was in the full realization of this act that, when the Cripps Mission failed, Generalissimo Chiang Kai-shek cabled to Mr. Churchill bluntly saying that China's life depended on renewed efforts to put India into the war on the side of the Allied Nations, and demanding, for the sake of our common cause, that conferences be resumed.

But, some say, let us not be so gloomy. The present policy in India may be completely successful. This I will declare frankly seems to me nothing but fantastic optimism. Nearly fifty thousand Indians are in jail. All those who could gather the people behind them are in jail.

But such facts change from time to time and place to place. One breakdown is patched up by force, and another occurs. The one all-important fact is that even though the present policy in India succeeds, it fails. How can a sullen, antipathetic, repressed people be our willing allies?

What our so-called realists will never understand is that man does not live by bread alone. All the forces of the body cannot be summoned until the force of the mind takes command, until the mind sees clearly the issue. And the mind has to believe that what it commands the body to fight for is worth the fight. Our bodies can be mobilized by law and police and men with guns, if necessary—but where shall we find that which will make us believe in what we must do, so that we can fight through to victory? Where is the clear call which alone can summon the soul?

It will not come until we seek it. There is no answer unless there is first a cry. There must be first the demand from us, before there will come the moral leadership necessary at this hour to take away our bafflement, and give us clear cold confidence in our cause.

6. CHINA FACES THE FUTURE

WHAT the future is which we all face, nobody knows. There are trends which if followed, might make the future as opposite to what we want as dictatorship is from democracy. Those trends are developing at fairly even paces today, and no one can say which one will begin to move more quickly, more widely, more deeply than another, or when there will cease to be this neck-and-neck race between the trends which make up our confusion.

I shall not begin, therefore, with the problematical future and what China may have to do with it. I am going to begin at the other end, with China's past, and through Chinese eyes, as far as I am able, I shall look toward the future, and gauge as far as I can China's influence upon it and her relation to it, in its various probabilities.

Of course no one looks to the future out of blank eyes. One faces the future with one's past—the body, born into a certain nation, part of a certain people, parcel of a certain civilization; the mind, stored with a certain experience, trained in a certain education. Thus Chinese eyes, looking at the future, will not see what

A lecture at the New School for Social Research, New York, October 13, 1942.

WHAT AMERICA MEANS TO ME

American eyes see, for our pasts are different. Let us review, in a few paragraphs, China's past, in the light of this moment at which we stand between yesterday and tomorrow.

We must remember, of course, that the Chinese people have basic differences from us. I always tell Chinese that to understand the people of the United States they must approach us not through our geographical or our political and religious divisions, but through the divisions into which our original races and national origins have put us. We have not yet escaped our original races and original nations. To understand the people of China we cannot approach them through racial origins, for they are roughly speaking one race. I have often told of a Chinese mother saying to me with pity in her eyes and voice, "How sorry I am for American women, because they never know what color eyes and hair their children will have!" Nor can we divide the Chinese people by their religions because they are so tolerant in their religious groups that one may be Confucian, Taoist and Buddhist at once—a tolerance which we will approach when we are willing for a man to be a Catholic and a Protestant at the same time. Nor can we know the Chinese through understanding their political divisions, for these are not yet fixed according to modern definitions.

Indeed, the Chinese are a singularly unified people. They are perhaps more united than any people on earth today. Their long history, lived out upon one piece of the globe's surface, their traditional lack of interest in expansion, either of land or power, have combined to tie them together in common family customs and common beliefs and habits. Even the furniture in the houses is arranged somewhat the same, wherever you are in north or south, and the architecture, though varied in detail, is in general everywhere the same, though the territory of China is roughly half again as large as that of the United States and her people roughly four times as many as ours.

We must then find China's division largely geographical. There are three main divisions in so-called China Proper, or the Eighteen Provinces. These eighteen provinces divide naturally into groups of six. The northern group is watered by the Yellow River and its tributaries, the central is fed by the Yangtze River, and there remain the southern provinces, four of which form the basin of the West River, which flows into the sea not far from Canton. Fukien and Chekiang alone lie outside the influence of the great rivers.

But it is not only the rivers which divide China from east to west into three parts. Great mountain ranges split China from north to south. The division has left the people who live on the high western plateaus different from those who have lived on the wide central and eastern plains. They are different chiefly for the reason that the eastern part of China has had access to the peoples across the sea and to that extent to what we call modern civilization. The Chinese locked between the mountains of China and of India have been isolated from these modern influences and have remained in a different time period from the rest of China. There has been, too, the influence upon those of the still more isolated tribes and peoples beyond China, and with whom they have intermarried to some extent. The isolation is more interesting when one remembers that this same region, particularly in the northwest, was once the cradle of Chinese civilization, played upon and shaped by contacts with Greece and Rome, Persia and Europe, through trade routes.

It is interesting, too, to know now, that this war has broken down the division. When the Japanese attacked from the east, the Chinese people began to move toward the west in that trek which is perhaps the greatest migration the human race has ever made. It is roughly estimated that fifty million people moved westward, and there is today taking place an amalgamation of China's people which centuries, perhaps, of peaceful life could not have accomplished. Indeed, had there been no such forced migration, it is quite possible that China, east and west, might have developed so separately that in time there would have been the equivalent of two peoples, varying so widely in their cultures that two separate nations would have been the result.

As it is, without in the least advocating war as a benefit, one may say that the war has forced together these two widely differing sections of China's people, both through the migration and also through the use of airplanes coming in from the west. The few planes which are now flying over the Himalayas from India cannot be considered of great importance in their cultural influence upon the people who today look up from their high lands and see them pass in the sky. But the fact that they are there means that there is communication with India and Europe. After this war, when without doubt airways will be more traveled everywhere than seaways or railways or highways, West China will no longer be the inaccessible territory she has been considered in the past. The old caravan road through Turkestan to Russia, too, is being traversed again, but now by trucks and planes overhead instead of by camel caravans. This is another link being freshly forged between the West and inner China, so long isolated because long ago ships took the trade away from camels.

Meanwhile Chinese from the east are growing acquainted with Chinese in the west. They are seeing countrymen of whom they have been almost as ignorant as the people of America are. This is an important potentiality for the further unification of China as a great single nation, no longer divided even by her natural geographical barriers. Indeed, it may be that the vast northwest, one third of China's territory, will one day be the center of her people, as it used to be. There are modern Chinese who are advocating that Lanchow, the capital of Kansu province, should be the capital of the China of the future, since it is equi-distant from Shanghai on the sea, Urga in Mongolia, and Tienhua in Sinkiang province.

The influence of geography upon people is always a tempting subject, but I dare not pursue it. The dry clear stimulating climate of north China has had its effect upon the people there and the soft humidity of the rich Yangtze valley has had a different effect, and so, too, has the semi-tropical heat of the West River territory. But basically these differences have been somewhat overcome by the length of time in which the Chinese have lived in China.

Let us now consider their time history. To put into a page or two an outline of four thousand years that the memory can hold, is perhaps of no particular use. At any rate, we will discard the legendary period and make it about three thousand years. Let us divide these three thousand years into five periods. First there was the

Feudal Age, which began roughly 1000 to 1500 years B.C. and ended about 200 B.C. in a period of disorder and warring states.

Out of these states came one who organized the nation again and we have the period of the First Empire, in two dynasties, the Ch'in and the Han, the Han being often called the period of China's Augustan Age. This lasted until 221 A.D. Decadence set in and warring leaders out of the people struggled together and the country was divided, in the period called The First Partition. In this period were first the three kingdoms of which we find the best picture in that great and ancient Chinese novel, *The Three Kingdoms,* translated into English by S. Brewitt Taylor. These kingdoms were combined into the Tsin dynasty, then divided into the Southern and Northern Empires, which brings us roughly to 600 A.D.

Then comes the fourth period, the Second Empire. It had first two dynasties, the Sui and the brilliant T'ang, the age of poets and painters. Five short dynasties followed, to reach about 1000 A.D. and then came the great Sung dynasty, which divided into the fifth period, the Second Partition. Upon the divided people of the Chin and Southern Sung dynasties, the Mongols descended, to found the Yuan or Mongol dynasty. It was the birth time of much that was new, as the rude strong Mongols poured their vitality into the perhaps over-civilized Chinese.

The Ming dynasty followed, a Chinese dynasty, which a Chinese monk began by overthrowing the quickly decadent Mongol emperors, who ruled less than a hundred years. Crude men become more quickly decadent than civilized men, it seems. The Ming dynasty lasted something less than three hundred years and was followed by a Manchurian dynasty, the Ching. It ended in 1911 with the establishment of a republic. China had her country back again.

Had the old Chinese pattern been followed, I suppose that Chiang Kai-shek would have been the founder of a new dynasty. The pattern of Chinese political history has always been the long upsweep of a dynasty, rising to an age of great brilliance and fine flowering, and thence declining quickly to decadence. At a certain stage discontent always broke out among the people and then there arose strong and vigorous men of the people who warred among themselves for the first place. The successful one founded a new dynasty. This explains the place of the war lord in Chinese history. The process was essentially democratic. A dynasty ruled as long as it could rule, and was taken over by the strongest man of the people. Sun Yat-sen broke the pattern by introducing the idea of a republic, an idea which nevertheless found a welcome among the always democratic-minded Chinese.

For whatever the dynasty the real rule in China has always belonged to the people. The Emperor stood to the people somewhat in the position that the Pope stands to Catholics. He was a spiritual head, an intermediary between the people and Heaven. But the people in the villages and the towns decided their own ways of life. There was no such conception of the State as we have now. The State did not prosecute, for example. A criminal was returned to his native place and judged by his own peers, and indeed by the members of his clan. A high sense of family honor usually made this judgment severe. The family took and still takes the place of the state, although the war will undoubtedly do much to change this in future China. The idea of a modern state is evolving very fast in China these days.

But the life of a people is the result not only of geography and history. It is the result, too, of their culture. If culture is shaped by the people, yet it also shapes the people, especially through so long a history as China has had. How can I put in a few words the essential difference between Chinese culture and our own? Perhaps the most vivid contrast is this—that China's individual great men have had more to do with shaping her culture than ours have had, and this because China, in her respect for the individual, has always given heed to her great men. If Chinese people have not had much respect for government or officials, and have cared little for the idea of a state, they have had the highest respect for a great man, and have given to their great men the sort of obedience which we have given to the state alone. Such individuals as Confucius and Lao-tse and Chuang-tse and Mo-tse and others have emerged from among the people because of their superior individual qualities. The people recognized their superiority and followed these great men and heeded their advice and shaped their conduct by the rules of behavior which such men laid down for them. Nor were these arbitrary rules. These great men were born out of the people and were products of their times, and they organized, made articulate the thoughts and feelings of the people, so that in a sense they explained the people to themselves. It was an eclectic process. The great men were in themselves the flower and fruit of China's culture, that culture which has always been and is today the culture of the common man. It is as if we followed Whitman and Emerson and Mark Twain and William James and

John Dewey and Carl Sandburg. The Chinese have approached democracy at the opposite pole from ours—that is, by the fostering of individualism, and not by fostering the mass.

This respect for the noble and the able individual meant that such individuals developed freely. Education was there to be had for all, but most people were not educated in the book sense. There were no public schools in old China, but there were many schools kept by scholars where fees were low and where anyone could be a pupil. Yet the Chinese saw no great use merely in knowing one's letters, and unless a boy showed extraordinary ability he was not encouraged to go to school and waste his time there. He was put to work. When there appeared a brilliant boy, however, not only his immediate family but the whole clan and sometimes a whole township or region would combine to pay for schooling and to give him every advantage, in order that he might bring them honor. He on his part felt this debt keenly, and exerted himself to the utmost to be worthy of all the sacrifice. Thus the unusual individual was not only born, but he was also developed in and by Chinese society. He was not only developed but he was also given respect as long as he lived and long after he died, so that genius in China was thus early discovered, assiduously fostered, and forever honored. It is no wonder that in such an atmosphere genius flourished not for its own sake, but for the sake of guiding the people by its superior intelligence, and that the culture of China benefited so greatly from the honor given to great individuals.

By this recognition of the superior individual, by this use of such an individual for the common good, Chinese democracy escaped a fallacy which has held back our own democracy. That is, China, although she believed as we do in the right of the common man to life and happiness, did not instill the notion that all men are born equal. Chinese have too much common sense for that. They recognized the fact that some are born with better brains and abilities than others, and upon the superior individuals were put the burden of higher development and special responsibility. A common man did not believe he could be emperor—or president. He knew that unless Heaven had endowed him with special natural gifts, he could not be.

I do not know of any country in the world except China where this attitude toward the gifted individual has been so universally adopted and so highly beneficial in its results upon society as a whole. The democratic feeling of the Chinese expresses itself rightly in the fact that these gifted individuals are expected as often—perhaps more often—in the homes of the simple and the honest and the poor as in the homes of the well-to-do. Their origin is never despised. Wherever they appear they receive honor. From such persons have come the crystallizations of the culture of China's people. Confucius was such a crystallizer, synthesizing as he did all that he felt and knew about his own people, and passing all this material through the process of his own extraordinary brain. These great men were born of the people, but because they crystallized what the people had been living and thinking, they carried the people on to a new life.

This is of course the process of individual genius in any civilization, but it had peculiar worth in China for two reasons. First, the long history of China's people is a particularly rich soil from which to spring; and second, the people themselves encouraged the development of genius by their attitude of respect and honor which they gave to the individual who possessed it.

The idea of genius, in the Chinese mind, always included moral worth. Men like Napoleon and Hitler did arise in China and their abilities were granted, but their lack of moral worth was considered a defect, and they never achieved a wide or permanent hold over the minds of the people. This emphasis upon moral worth continues in China today as strongly as ever. Chinese men and women on the whole are no better and no worse than the average of other peoples. They are not more moral than other people. And yet that belief in the necessity of goodness, at least in those whom they honor and follow, prevails even where the moral principles are not followed by the people or by other individuals. A man may be a bad man, but he will accept the fact that he is a bad man as a defect. And a good man is praised and believed in. There is a value to a people in maintaining standards of moral worth, even when these standards often are frankly abandoned. I think the Chinese people are perhaps more free from hypocrisy of the self-deceiving sort than any people I know.

I repeat, to illustrate what I mean, my favorite example. I once was in a temple whose priests were notoriously evil, and an old man came in to worship. When he had finished we fell into talk and I asked him, "Does it disturb you in your worship that the priests here are known not to be worthy followers of Buddha?" He looked at me surprised and said, "Shall I not believe in God because some men are evil?" That is, the average Chinese will not cease to believe in the reality and value of goodness because there are many not good. The effect of this belief is a moral strength to the nation. It has had a special strength when the Chinese have demanded of their great men that they also be good, and have said that in so far as a man is not good, he falls short of greatness.

So the great men of China, infused with goodness and encouraged by popular demand for goodness, have in turn occupied themselves with the welfare of the common people. Confucius spent his entire time and thought on consideration of the common man, his relationships and the especial responsibility of the Emperor and others in authority to that common man. The *lao pei hsing*, as the common man is called in China, has always been a matter of concern for those above. Even evil rulers have made a feint of doing good to the people. When times grew decadent, the common people have been often oppressed in China, and when times were disordered, as they always were between dynasties and as they were during the years when the republic was being established, there was much oppression of the people, mainly by little men newly risen to power. But when this happened everybody knew it was wrong and especially the people knew it was wrong, and they made a noise about it. So all through oppression and injustice the ideal of the common's man good has remained unchanged. When local officials or gentry oppressed those in their region, it might go on for a while but the noise of it went abroad.

I will give a current example. Generalissimo Chiang Kai-shek recently made a journey into the northwest where, he reported, the situation of the people was on the whole satisfactory, but there were cases in which local gentry, and even public authorities, had been hoarding grain, raising prices, and oppressing the people. Such cases he directed to be reported to him, and if they were hushed up by the local authorities, these authorities would be held to blame and punished. In other words, the Generalissimo is simply carrying on the tradition of his country in making it known that the people are to have access to him in cases of injustice. This does not of course take the place, and ought not to take the place of proper courts of law; but where the people can appeal to their ruler it shows that the case of the people against their oppressors is a matter for concern to the ruler.

This attitude toward the common man has had important results. It has made the Chinese ordinary man articulate and independent. He considers himself of value to the nation. Many travelers in China have remarked upon the upright free carriage of the average man there, and his air of self-respect whatever his job and position. This is the result of the respect that he has been given as a man, for centuries. Another important result is that at this moment, when it is still not clear what sort of a war this is, the Chinese people see it as a people's war, and believe that only as a people's war will it be fought and won.

China will doubtless go the way of all nations, as her industries develop after the war. The common man there will have his problems with employers, with labor unions and all the rest of it. But he will have as his aids these two facts—the long respect that Chinese civilization has accorded sincere moral worth, and the long respect it has accorded the people—that is, the common man.

Nowhere is the contrast greater between Chinese and Japanese civilization than upon these very points. Japan has never valued the individuals in her society. Japan has not followed her great men, but her governments. As a result, she has not developed many great men. Japan has never considered moral worth to be of high value, but has substituted the empty forms of emperor worship and chauvinistic patriotism. Japan has never valued the common man, but has considered him merely as material for the dreams of chauvinists and warriors. It is strange that almost side by side these two utterly different civilizations should have existed, and for centuries. When Japan went to China to borrow of her civilization she brought back much, but she did not bring back that beneficent humanism which was personified in Chinese belief in good and great individuals and in the worth of the common man. Japan, that is, did not look for nor find the heart of Chinese civilization. In a way, these two eastern peoples personify the conflicting forces in the world today and have personified them for centuries in their two ways of life.

So much for the sort of past out of which the Chinese have come, the solid past upon which they stand so firmly today, ready to face the future.

How does China face the future? Let me answer this question first through Generalissimo Chiang Kai-shek. He is fond of quoting to his people that they must face ten thousand changing circumstances with an unchanging self. He has become in China today a sort of legend to the people. He is a combination of great man and ruler, and the people look to their ruler as they look also to a great man.

Nobody has yet written a book which really explains Chiang Kai-shek. He was born in simple circumstances; his mother was a widow, and he was a poor boy, though his family was respectable. He did not have much education, as education goes nowadays, and there are periods in his youth and middle years which are not a credit to him. But there is real greatness in the man and the Chinese value him by the greatness. The greatness has brought him through to a position of high moral worth today. He is criticized, I know, for condoning corruption in high places and very near him. Again, his policy here is one which the Chinese people understand and value. He is not ignorant of the corruption, and when a man's corruption becomes greater than his worth to China, that man goes. But it is typical of the Chinese attitude toward moral worth that Chiang understands how rarely complete goodness is found, and he knows he must work often with imperfect tools, for few men are entirely honest. The Chinese are shrewd and wise, and never cynical. Only young peoples are cynical. Chiang Kai-shek personifies for the Chinese people today, both as great man and as ruler, that unchanging self, with which they face so calmly the ten thousand changing circumstances of the future.

But what is the future which China, which all of us, face? Who can tell? One can only guess roughly that it will probably take one of three possible shapes, any of which may be definite or modified.

The horrible possibility of Axis victory we must instantly dismiss. Yet the Chinese are realists and they know they must prepare against that possibility. Should the Axis win the war, then China would have to maintain herself as she has in the past, her essential nature penetrating in all possible ways the alien life that has come into her. She would seem to adapt herself outwardly, but inwardly she would yield nothing, and in the end those who had taken her would be taken. This is the process of centuries, but surer in the end than any other form of conquest.

There is the possibility of clear victory for the democracies, coming more quickly than we dare today to hope, coming so quickly that the essential forms of democracy may yet remain unchanged. If victory comes as quickly as this for the United Nations, it will have come too quickly for us to have changed at all. In that case there would still be an unchanged imperialism in Asia, and unchanged relations between the man of England and the United States and the man of Asia. It is fortunate for the world that China is fighting on the allied side and is cutting across the color line in this war. China has never thought primarily in terms of color. Nevertheless, this does not mean that she will go on enduring the disadvantages of color prejudice, which she considers ridiculous. China will insist on a future where progress toward human cooperation will not be blocked by color prejudices and by the superiority-inferiority relationships of imperial rule. If the war does not bring about certain fundamental changes for the future, then China believes that peace must bring them.

But sudden victory either for ourselves or the Axis is improbable. China faces a future much more likely to be a changed democracy, changed in one of two ways.

This war will be won by the democracies either as a totalitarian war or as a people's war. We cannot hope to win it in our present undecided divided fashion. Either it will be won as a people's victory or as a people's defeat. If it is to be a people's defeat, even though a military victory for the United Nations, then the evils which we fight in our enemies today will be in ourselves, to be attacked and destroyed one by one as the people have the strength to do so.

Since China will herself remain unchanged, or certainly less changed than the rest of us, she will then have to face a future where even the triumphant democracies, her allies, are no longer democracies. She will have to live with them, but without yielding up her self.

It is only if we decide to make this a people's war—that is, if we decide to go all out for democracy, and declare that freedom and human equality shall be *our* unchanged self—that China can feel at ease about the future and give her whole heart and strength to the winning of the war, sure that peace will be peace, and not simply a continuing of the war for democracy—that is, the right of people to be born free and equal to each other.

For China is fighting this war not primarily as our ally. She is fighting this war because she believes in freedom and human equality. She does not want to be dominated by anybody, nor does she want to be looked down upon by anybody because her people are Oriental and have yellow skin and black eyes and hair. She wants her people to have a place in the human race equal to that of any other people, and she makes this a principle She is our ally because she will not be dominated by anyone, not even by another yellow-skinned, black-haired, black-eyed people. She is for freedom, regardless of race and color. She will be our ally so long as we take the same stand, and so far as we take the same stand. This is her unchanging self which faces the changing future.

No more domination, an equal chance for everybody, and cooperation *with* instead of rule *over* must be the law of relationships between people. China takes this stand in sensible self-interest, which she believes will be the self-interest of all. But it is a moral stand, too, and China is not afraid of the word moral anywhere. Perhaps the most frequently used word in her simple vocabulary is the word which expresses it—the word *li*, which means to behave rightly in all relationships.

This *li*, or sense of the fitting and right behavior in human relationships, will be, I believe, China's greatest contribution to the future. When this war ends in a victory for the United Nations, the statesmen with their experts and advisors will gather about the peace table to decide the future of the whole world. You remember that peace table after the first world war. China was not there. An Englishman, an American, a Frenchman and an Italian sat there and the wretched peace treaty they made was no peace treaty at all.

This time there will be no question of China's presence at the peace table. I believe that it will be the saving of the peace that she will be there. For China has a wisdom in human relationships that none of us has. She has a good sense that none of us has. She will know that if a treaty contains in it the seeds to germinate another war, it will not be a peace treaty. However much she has suffered, she will have the sense not to want to suffer any more, and to plan ways for all of us of avoiding more suffering. China has lived so long that she has learned what newer peoples have not—she has learned how to learn from mistakes.

To that peace table let us hope that China will be allowed to bring her unchanged self, that self which has already lived through ten thousand changes, and can live through ten thousand more.

CHINA FACES THE FUTURE

For that unchanging self will in itself change the future, and to the benefit of all mankind. The emphasis upon moral worth in our great men, how sorely we need that emphasis today! Our great men, our leaders, need to have impressed upon them, by the demand of the people, that they be men of moral worth, and as men of moral worth, that they realize afresh their responsibility for the welfare of the common man. Nazism has destroyed the necessity for moral worth as it has destroyed the value of the common man. Evil men rise up and seize the power and make a boast of their evil. To this China will help us oppose the unchanging principle that there can be no greatness without goodness as an essential quality in it.

Perhaps the wisdom of China's people can be made the wisdom of the world, that wisdom which listens to its great and good men first, and shapes governments according to what it hears, instead of as Japan has done, and as modern Nazis do, who compel the people to brutal blind obedience of governments established and maintained by evil force. Perhaps China's age-long belief in the value of the common man and the responsibility of all toward him and for his welfare may be made a foundation upon which our future will rest.

In a word, China's attitude toward the future is the result of her past. She brings to the future an attitude of enlightened humanism, a belief that individual man, and not the machine, is the most important thing in the world. If she can bring this unchanging self to the future, perhaps we who are the people of the world outside China may be saved from the horrors of the machine we have made and from the rule of that machine over our lives.

WHAT AMERICA MEANS TO ME

I do not know how far China realizes her own potentiality in shaping the future. She has not been encouraged, I am sure, by the way in which she is now being treated. The men in power in this war, the military men, the political men, are men ignorant of the Chinese. It can scarcely be hoped that they will be less ignorant after this war. I am not afraid of China's changing but I am greatly afraid that the help she might give at the peace table, and in shaping the world after it, may be lost because of the ignorance of our leaders.

In this case I can only appeal to the American people that they do not remain ignorant. The American people must somehow be brought to realize that in the people of China we have an ally, not only for waging this war, but even more for the waging of the inevitable conflicts of peace. This war will not insure to us the benefits or the rights of democracy. Let us cement now our friendship with the Chinese people, who perhaps more than any other on earth, because of their long experience in democracy, can help us the most in the future.

7. RELIEF—FOR THE AMERICAN CONSCIENCE

MANY years ago, when I was a young girl in China, a certain winter came when I was old enough, my mother said, no longer to be shielded from the sorrows of life.

We lived in a modest mission bungalow in the country outside the large river port of Chinkiang. Ours was a prosperous region, at the junction of the Yangtse river and the Grand Canal. Down the canal that winter suddenly came thousands of refugees from the north where the crops had failed. It was a new sight to see those hordes of starving people pour into our streets with their children and their old. They were frantic with hunger and they begged unashamed and too often they lay down and died before they could be fed. The sorrow from which I was not to be shielded was the worst famine China had known in a generation.

My parents gave up all their regular work and devoted themselves to the refugees. The wealthy Chinese, too, opened rice kitchens. But all that we could do was not enough. My father and his associates said grimly that we must cable to America for food and for funds. They

An article published in *The New York Times Magazine,* January 10, 1943.

WHAT AMERICA MEANS TO ME

did, and with wonderful generosity the food and funds came.

It was my first experience of what my own people could do and I was proud of it. I remember telling hungry Chinese when I gave them their dole, "This is from America—the Americans sent this—" and with what pride I heard their heartfelt replies, "Ah, America is good—the Americans have good hearts!"

So I grew up loving the generosity of my fellow countrymen, accepting it with joyous faith when I was on the receiving end in China. But during the last two years I have worked on the giving end of this relief business, here in America, and some curious questions have sprung at me. I have watched the people in our cities and towns and in little country villages putting their hands into their pockets and taking out their dollars and their dimes for Chinese war relief. It is a wonderful sight, a sight to be seen nowhere else in the world.

But why is it that we continue thus to pour out relief? When we analyze it we find that our relief is not for all the hungry but only for the hungry ones whom we like. In Asia we enjoy feeding the Chinese, but who can rouse any interest among us in feeding the hungry of India? The people of India are infinitely poorer than the people of China and eighty per cent of them are continually underfed. I doubt whether any sort of relief could be raised for India, even with England's consent. I don't see any relief organizations for the starving millions of Puerto Rico, for whose suffering we are really responsible. It is evidently not a feeling of pure humanity which prompts our relief; it is something else.

Now the average practical Chinese reasons that it is unnatural for a people to send millions of dollars to

RELIEF—FOR THE AMERICAN CONSCIENCE

other people they have never seen, never expect to see, and apparently—considering the Asiatic exclusion laws—never want to see. Why do we give millions for Chinese relief with such joy, when we will not even allow a hundred odd Chinese a year to enter our country on an immigration quota, and when we make the entry into this country even of highborn Chinese such torture that they have been known to commit suicide in despair over long and hopeless detention at our gates? There is a curious contradiction here that has to be examined.

And why we have become more and more complacent about the known fact that China is being steadily relegated to a lesser place among our allies? We hear without public protest that China is suffering desperately for want of a few airplanes. Five hundred modern airplanes, responsible Chinese tell us, would enable them to beat back the Japanese advance. Our monthly output of planes is in the thousands. But still the planes scarcely trickle to China.

When we feel uneasily that we are not being fair to China as a war ally, the relief funds shoot up another million dollars, and we feel better. The Chinese ought really to be grateful to us, of course, for so much relief. But I shall be worried if very soon China does not begin to ask for something more than relief. She has been asking but in mild and polite terms. There is in Washington a military representative direct from Generalissimo Chiang, and he has been asking for war planes, but he is not heard outside of Washington, and who in Washington hears anything?

Chinese representatives do not sit in the councils of major war strategy in Washington, nor have they been regarded as equals in any way in this war, nor is there the slightest sign yet that they will be given an equal place at the peace table, or in the planning of the future world. We have let China deteriorate into a sort of appendage to the war alliance which we have made primarily with Britain, and after Britain maybe with Russia. We have made up our minds that though we love China we are not going to let love interfere with business, and so instead of a proposal of real alliance with China, we are going to send flowers in the form of relief.

But money for relief does not in the slightest degree compensate for such facts as that Burma was lost, because China's agonized plea to be allowed to defend it was unheeded until it was too late to do anything except to allow three crack divisions of Chinese troops to be destroyed. Nor will relief money compensate for the loss of India, if that loss comes, for China then will be completely isolated, from relief as well as from all else.

What is wrong is that while we really are a sincere, good, kind people, we hate to have our brains stirred. We are very bad at human relationships. We feel we cannot bother about that sort of thing. We are too busy to try to find out how the fellow across the ocean—or next door—feels or what he wants. We will do anything rather than get ourselves involved in something requiring more than physical action. That is perhaps one reason why we are urgent about winning this war before we talk about peace. War can be won with physical energy. Peace cannot. We take it that any international goodwill we need can be purchased more easily and quickly by relief money and by our superiority in technical skills and by trade, than by the difficult and tedious business of having to understand and approach human

RELIEF—FOR THE AMERICAN CONSCIENCE

beings through their minds and hearts, especially if they cannot speak our language.

So when I hear Chinese men and women wondering why we pour out our good money in relief, and solving the puzzle by concluding that we are soft-hearted and also a little soft-headed, I know they are right in what they say, though not in what they mean.

We are soft-hearted toward the Chinese because we like them. We are soft-headed because we do not want to face the fundamental causes of why they suffer. We lull our brains with our own money. We try to compensate for what we don't want to do, by doing what we are willing to do—give money. We give the Chinese a piece of bread, when what they want is a good hard stone to heave at the enemy. The old saying works both ways.

It costs trouble and pain and time to go to the bottom of a human problem and work on causes. It takes study and thought and cooperation. We as a people do not like to study, thought bores us, and we fear cooperation with people we don't know. It terrifies us to think of cooperating even with the Chinese whom we like.

We Americans can be very fond of people without for one moment thinking of equality with them. Indeed, we are rather more fond of them for that reason. If China wants relief money from us more than she wants equality as our ally in the war and a partner in peace, all she has to do is to be grateful for the relief we send, and by her gratitude make us feel generous. If China does this, I shall be frightened, not for China but for us. Whatever the Chinese are, they are not stupid. If they want money from us more than anything else, it means something unpleasant and dangerous for the world. In spite of all Japan's ructions, and in spite of Chiang Kai-shek's noble repudiation of the leadership of Asia, China cannot help but be the leader of Asia, yesterday and today, and maybe forever. We had better count on that and plan accordingly. China is no child to be forever satisfied with our animal crackers sent in the form of relief.

What nags my brain is this: Why do we think giving relief will establish goodwill, when relief is not what any self-respecting people really wants? One has to feed people starving in an emergency, but after one feeds one goes on to the real job, which is getting the works going so that there will not be such emergencies. No amount of relief can buy goodwill anywhere, and we had better not be so silly as to think it will.

It does not purchase good will either in the one who gives or in the one who receives. There was a time when the relief hullabaloo was about the poor Armenians, and our generation has never been able to respect the Armenians as they deserve. During the first world war children heard a great deal about relief for the poor Belgians. I think that generation has never wholly respected the Belgians since. Today our children are besought to save their pennies for the "poor Chinese." At this I rebel. The Chinese are not "poor." They are a strong, brave, superior people, and I don't want my children growing up thinking they are poor. I want my children to grow up thinking of Chinese as their equals, not as people fit only for charity. No relationship between our two great democracies can grow out of that sort of thinking.

Whenever there is any serious talk about getting to work with China and other nations now to organize the world against starvation and aggression, the hush-hushers, now in the seats of the mighty, tell us, "The war must be won first." Won for what—so that we can be

RELIEF—FOR THE AMERICAN CONSCIENCE

Santa Claus again, for pure self indulgence? The sooner we Americans get over wanting to be Santa Claus, the better it will be. The world is growing up. Everywhere the peoples are coming to believe that the world can be so organized that they can work for what they get and contribute their own share to the world's well being.

Of course immediate relief to the suffering countries must not stop. But we must see it for what it is, an emergency measure, a partial measure, to be carried on with the left hand while the right hand and the brains do the work of real world reconstruction, the work of making China and all other countries units in a functioning whole.

We Americans are taking refuge in relief. By this by-play we are excusing ourselves from what must be done in real work. We are enjoying the luxury of being generous in small ways, while we refuse the one great gift which alone will save those whom we keep on our charity lists.

What is the great gift? It is the determination to undertake our share, not only with our money but with our brains and our energy and our spiritual integrity, to bring about a cooperation of all nations in a world where the gifts of charity will no longer be needed to palliate the deep ills of the peoples.

8. THE SPIRIT BEHIND THE WEAPON

THE divisions among and between peoples of the world form always a curious criss-cross pattern. There is no one way of dividing us. We are different races, and that is a division. We are different nations, and that is a division. Religion is a division, and wealth is a division and education is a division. Climate and geography and food have their dividing effects, and so has history.

But war is the great simplifier. In times of war people put aside their lesser differences and return to their primary divisions. From these, as from fortresses, they wage war.

Yet the fortresses from which men fight are not the same from war to war. In the last World War, the primary division among people was still the old one of nations. The dying words of Edith Cavell, "Patriotism is not enough," were a prophesy of this greater war in which we are today involved. But patriotism was almost enough in that World War. We fought it as an international struggle and after the truce was declared we retired again into our nations and built the walls high between.

An article published in *Survey Graphic*, November, 1942.

THE SPIRIT BEHIND THE WEAPON

Nevertheless, all through the too brief years of the truce, great heaving changes took place. Nations became less and less important, and peoples more and more important. The revolution in Russia destroyed a nation and hewed out, by the crudest and sometimes the most cruel means, a people. The revolution in China destroyed another nation and built upon the ancient foundations another people. That the revolution in China was mainly political and certainly disturbed the foundations less severely than in Russia, was evidence of the already fundamentally democratic character of the Chinese.

But it is always true that when great changes occur among human beings, there is an instant strengthening, too, of the old. Thus old Japan awoke and laid its hard hand upon the new people there. It was inevitable that the awakening of the life of the people in Japan was more slow than either in Russia or China, for nationalism was more deeply established in Japan than in these other two countries. The people in Japan were long integrated into a nation, as they were in France yesterday and are in England today. Had the Japanese new people been allowed a little longer to live, had the last war been revolutionary rather than reactionary in its effects, this second war might never have followed. But since the last war reestablished the nation-unit, only the countries relatively untouched by the war escaped the reaction. The fact that in Europe and America peoples retired into their nations gave strength to old Japan to emerge and to crush the rising of her own new people. Japan is fighting this present war as a nation, and as a nation she will lose it. Whether she will lose it as a people remains to be seen. China is fighting this war as a people, and so is Russia, and these two peoples will win this war.

The United States is both a nation and a people. It is our deepest division. There are those who insist that we must fight this war as a nation, and these refuse to see the war except as an encroachment upon our soil and trade. There are also those who know that we can only hope to win if we fight it as a people, and these know that it is necessary that freedom live in the atmosphere of the world if our own freedom is to be assured.

But this strange awful war is little enough understood by any of us. Why are we fighting? What brought us into this mortal combat? It was not merely that Japan attacked us at Pearl Harbor, for why did Japan attack us? It was not merely that Hitler rose to threaten the world in Europe. Why did Hitler rise and why was he able to rise? Those who would attribute the war to such superficial occasions as an attack and an uprising are romantically inclined. Realism compels us to seek further. The real roots of this war, I believe, are deep in the essential difference between those who cling to the old concept of the nation as the division unit of mankind and those who see the new concept of the peoples. Or put it otherwise, this war is the result of the necessity, at this period in man's development, for changing our nation-unit for mankind into a larger people-unit.

What compels the change? Primarily, perhaps, the discovery of the universalities of science. Science has, more than any other thing, taught us to think in terms of the universe. The very business of working with scientific methods, of thinking in scientific terms, as well as the fruits of science, have led us to universality. The scientifically mechanical means which have brought nations

THE SPIRIT BEHIND THE WEAPON

close together physically have at the same time destroyed the mental and spiritual boundaries of those nations, so that today there are people in many nations who are closer together, through their ideas and their feelings and desires—through their temperaments in a word—than they are to other persons of their own nation and race. The passing of physical barriers has enabled these persons to find each other. They are not limited, any more, to one nation. If today, therefore, we seek to make nationhood the chief division of man and the chief cause for which we fight this war, we are doomed to fail, for too many have found a larger cause.

What then? Are we to do away with nations? Certainly not. All of us need a physical home to love and cherish, to improve and beautify. All of us, for conveniences in daily life, if for nothing else, need a sound and useful local political organization. There would be chaos if there were no nations and no national governments. But to insist that nations must be the chief groups of mankind is today to insist that a small province ought to have been the limit of a man's thought yesterday, when already he thought in nations. Today, man's thought includes the globe.

And yet as in every change, there are some whose minds belong to yesterday, and these will try with all their strength to force us back. It is a very stubborn strength, since stubbornness and lack of perceptive imagination are almost invariably teammates. The mind that only knows what it has seen is the mind that arrogates to itself, too, the valuable attribute of realism. But realism is not to be found in the reactionary mind, which lives in a dream of the past. The old gospelites, who sing of the religion that was good enough for their fathers and therefore good enough for them, are, whatever their religion, simply not good enough for today and certainly not good enough for victory. If arms could win any war, they might be able to win this war, for yesterday's men can handle a gun and shoot it off as well as anybody. Unfortunately it takes wit and wisdom as well as a gun to win this war.

For this war, as has often been said, is revolution as well as war. We can recognize this fact today to our advantage or we can recognize it tomorrow to our cost. The word "revolution" has taken on evil accumulations because it has been so often accompanied by hateful acts. But stripped of those hateful acts, it means simply a great change. A revolution of people means a great change in and among people.

How can we use this fact about the present war to our advantage today? First by recognizing it, and this recognition implies that we recognize that our enemies are not certain nations, but certain people and that our allies, too, are certain people. Our enemies are those who refuse to allow freedom to be the atmosphere of the world, and who would instead set up one nation or one race over another. Our allies are those who demand the atmosphere of freedom and human equality for all. This is the way of life that the American people have chosen as theirs, the way which believes in the right of people to be born free and to be treated equally. A century and a half ago certain Americans expressed this way of life in words, and by and large, faltering and evading and staggering forward slowly and yet sometimes moving swiftly forward, too, we have held to that ideal as our own. It is not the way of life of our nation. A great many of our national laws and habits deny it. Many persons within

THE SPIRIT BEHIND THE WEAPON

our nation refuse to follow it, and do not accept it as their way of life, but still enough of the people believe it and try to follow it, so that it remains our chosen way.

But it is not only the American way. It is also the Chinese way. Long before any American put the way into words, Chinese had put it into words. Today there are people in many nations who have chosen this way of life and who have put it into words. Russia, with bloodshed and contradiction, has put it into practice, imperfect but actual. Indians in India are trying to put it into practice.

In England there is the same division that there is in us between those who believe in freedom for all and those who try to put national and geographical boundaries to it. Churchill put such boundaries when he declared the Atlantic Charter did not apply to the British colonial possessions. Those words must be unsaid before we can hope to win this war, for if we cling to them we shall be fighting in yesterday and not today.

Men's minds cannot fight in yesterday and win, however modern the weapon in their hands. Hitler has proved that to us, if we needed proof. For Hitler's great weakness is that he has led his people into narrow nationhood at a moment when the peoples of the world are ready to move forward out of nationhood. There are peculiar reasons for Germany's backwardness. Her nationhood was not achieved at a time when it should have been achieved, so that now she has not had the experience of nationalism which the other nations have had, and which a people must experience, it seems, before they can find the liberation of passing beyond nationality.

The United States, on the other hand, went through a

forcing process. The necessity for national unity in a new and dangerous land compelled us early to be a nation. Then, too, there was enough land for all of us and we could build our nation free of the competition of cramped space and old and conflicting history. We had the chance to make a nation out of whole cloth, and to cut and fit it to our own shape. Germany has been long building a nation out of bits and scraps of used stuffs. But indeed the problems of Germany have been the problems of Europe. Europe has been frozen into nations. Peoples have never been able to pass beyond those units, and it may be that their eternal conflicts are basically due to that fact, and their struggle to develop beyond it. Mentally and spiritually the peoples of Europe have long been far beyond the boundaries of jealous nations, but physically they have been forced to remain in them, new wine continually being poured into old vessels.

Our own history is not so much like that of Europe as it is like that of Asia. The peoples of Asia have had wide lands, free spaces, and few national conflicts. The peoples of Asia are thinking in terms of people. Nation is not important to any of them. China is the Chinese people, India is the people of India, Russia is the people of Russia. That India and Russia have great variety among their peoples is of no significance today when nationhood increasingly means simply a political and organizational convenience.

We differ in one important regard, however, from the peoples of Asia. Race has never been a cause for any division among those peoples. But race prejudice divides us deeply, and hampers more than anything else our development toward a free people in a free world.

THE SPIRIT BEHIND THE WEAPON

For there is a solid part of our own American people who will not sacrifice, even for the sake of victory in this war, their prejudices against color. They had rather yield to Hitler than to give up their belief in the necessity for the white man to be supreme. We had better know this and speak it out clearly; for Hitler is already counting on the argument that all white men ought to join together against Japan in order to maintain white supremacy in the world, and we have those who will betray us all when Hitler dares to come forward with his proposals, which would spare him defeat at our hands. In that day those among us who would sacrifice our victory rather than their race prejudices will be those who will speak, not openly for Hitler, it is true, but for the old nation-unit. They will talk as patriots, but they will be Hitler's henchmen. If Hitler is counting on our race prejudice to help him, Japan also counts on it to help her persuade the peoples of Asia that we are still thinking in terms of nationhood and that we do not care for peoples. She is persuading the people of Burma and Malaya, and she is trying to persuade the people of India.

For fascism, hiding behind color prejudice, now threatens America; and what today threatens America, threatens the world. I can therefore see nothing but acute danger in the mental isolationist who insists that it is not our business what happens to the people of China or the people of India, or that what we do about the Negro here is not the business of the peoples abroad. The way we behave to our own colored people, like the way England behaves toward India, is the criterion by which we are judged by foe and ally alike.

And yet it is not too late for America to come forth by her own strength, if we can face with determination

WHAT AMERICA MEANS TO ME

the true meaning of today's war. This war is the primary conflict between the concept of national supremacy, and this includes racial supremacy, and the concept of the equality of peoples in a free world.

If this seems simplification, let us not be afraid of simplicity. It is only the strong who dare to be simple, who dare to reduce great problems to their essentials. Let us not be deceived by complexity. Too many escape into complexity these days. For it is an escape for persons to cry, when this question of the equality of peoples is raised in India or in our own South, "Ah, but the situation is not so simple."

Why are we afraid of simplicity? Simple questions go deep and the answers, if they are honest, go deeper still. With history as our guide and life as our experience, we ought by now to know that no great stride forward is ever made for the individual or for the human race unless the complex situation is reduced to one simple question and its simple answer. In our own history when the time came for us to declare our freedom, there were complexities as grave in proportion to the age and the population as ours are now. Had we listened to those persons who in 1776 were afraid of simplicity—and there were many—we should never have become a nation. In those days a few men gathered up the tangles of fearfulness and doubt into their clenched right fists and asked the simple question, "Shall we endure injustice, or shall we be free?" There were enough people who could answer as simply, "We will be free." And we were free.

There was another moment in our history, again in proportion to the times as complex as now, when the whole economic and social structure of the South and in a measure of the country was dependent upon slave la-

THE SPIRIT BEHIND THE WEAPON

bor. The Union rocked in division. But again there were those who stood up amid all the complexities and put the simple question, "Can our Union be worthy of free men when we hold human beings as slaves?" And there were enough Americans then to answer as simply, "We cannot have slavery in America." And the Union was saved.

The time has come for simplicity again. Can our people continue a free people in a world of peoples not free? The answer is inevitably, No.

How shall we win this war then for the freedom of peoples? We can win it only by sacrificing everything we have which denies that for which we fight. This sacrifice we have not yet been willing to make. Yet spiritually we are still in the phase in which we were materially a few months ago, when we were trying to keep our creature comforts and fight the war, too. We have found out that it cannot be done. We know now that most of the money we make and the food we eat and the clothes we wear and the furniture we would like to buy and the pleasure trips we would like to take have to be given up, and we have given them up. Materially we are ready for an all-out war effort.

But spiritually we are not. We still want to win this war, keeping all the spiritual clutter to which we have clung in times past. We want to let the muddle in our minds stand while we fight. We want to freeze our souls until after the war.

It cannot be done. No great war can be won without the spirit behind the weapons. The mind must be clear and the soul free before men can fight a war for freedom and win it. It is now time, therefore, and high time to see what we are willing to give up to win this war for the freedom of our people in a free world. First of all there must be the sacrifice of race prejudice. To harbor race prejudice in our own people automatically puts us on the wrong side. We fail in our leadership today, both at home and abroad, because of the contradiction our race prejudice puts upon freedom of peoples. I have it from as widely differing sources as Yale and the University of California that the contradiction is resulting in apathy toward the war on the part of young men now being drafted. It is producing doubt and apathy in millions abroad who would otherwise be our willing allies.

And yet it is obvious that the sacrifice of prejudice will be far more difficult than any material sacrifice. The government was able to help us make the material sacrifices by simply taking things away from us. But no democratic government can forbid a man his own will, or what he thinks, as it can forbid him his share of sugar and gas and rubber. A man's will remains his own and his feelings remain his own and his thoughts and his speech remain his own—at least in a democracy. Government may, by passing laws against discrimination and by urging us to remember that our allies are mostly colored, try to help us control our prejudices, but that is all it can do. It cannot dig into us and force out of us the traitorous wish and the determination not to yield up those prejudices, even to win the war. Whether that is done depends upon individual loyalty. Soul by soul only the individual soul can do it.

And yet, I say again, there are such souls. They live in England and they live here. Somehow we must make them known to the doubting peoples of the East, to our own discouraged colored people in the United States, to our apathetic young men.

THE SPIRIT BEHIND THE WEAPON

I do not believe much in the possibility of change in the individual human heart. Those who will not give up their prejudices which endanger our war effort far more than hoarding and bootlegging forbidden materials, will probably not change. The mind that doggedly insists on prejudice often has not intelligence enough to change. Then let us marshal the other minds and prove to our allies in India and China and everywhere in the world that at least there is a sufficient number of other white people, who will no longer tolerate imperialism and human inequality, to warrant the colored peoples throwing in their lot with the democracies now. It is the only hope left to bring these peoples to our side, and without them we cannot win this war. There may be another truce, but without them there can be no victory.

It is time for us to remember that today Japan is master of more of the world than we are, and that Japan is not white. Whether we like it or not, race has ceased to be a human division, and it is the realist's duty to proclaim the truth. All the stubbornness of the minds that live in the past will not remove the truth from the earth. They may spend their lives in struggle against it, but the truth goes marching on. The world now belongs no more to a nation or to a race. The war is between two kinds of people. As yet we people of America are fighting on both sides and against each other. How can we win a war for freedom until we mend this division?

No man, it is true, can cut himself off clean and instantly from his past. No change among people comes in a moment's time. There are those who must die and those who must be born. They die and they are born. If there were no war, we might wait for the process of time to do its work—teaching the generations as they appear, allowing nature to destroy prejudice by her secret slow intermingling.

Yet there is a special plea to be made now for a swifter process. Many valuable young lives will be lost unnecessarily if those who lead us do not understand what sort of a war this is. If they fight this war as they fought the war yesterday, we may lose our whole generation of young men. For it is now apparent that it is our young men who must bear the brunt of the fighting. It is a war in which we are using our youth in our battle line. They are reckless and strong, they are easily trained. And so they make very good soldiers. But still it would be well for our nation that they are not all lost, and the only hope that they will not all be lost in a prolonged war is in this one possibility—that those who lead us will see this war for what it is and will fight it for what it is—a war of one kind of people against another.

There is the real war. We fight it in every nation and on every soil. While our armies and navies and air fleets swarm over the world, we Americans at home must not for one moment lose sight of the real war, lest our youth be killed uselessly in Europe and England, in Burma and Australia, in China and the South Seas, in the Middle East and in Africa.

This is a war between peoples and the battlefield is everywhere.

9. THE CHANGING WAR

ENOUGH has happened since early December, 1941, to make five years. We were then in the long shadow of war, but hoping by some miracle to escape it. We knew that we were doomed, but we could not yet accept the doom. Our country was like a ship upon the ocean where the sun still shone, and although we were headed straight into the stormy sky ahead, it was hard to believe that those shadows were inevitable.

And yet human history has proved again and again that nothing is more inevitable than war when no steps are taken to prevent its coming. It came upon us, the shadow fell, and we are deep in that shadow now.

I am not a pacifist. I am a fatalist but only to this degree—that a certain fate is inescapable, either upon the individual or the nation, or the world, when that fate is not early foreseen and the course sharply changed to avoid it. Fate can be escaped only when it has not yet become fate—that is, when there is still an alternative. The passive mind accepts fate because it is not able or willing to take the trouble to face this alternative. Fate proceeds inexorably, therefore, only upon the passive

An address delivered at a dinner given for Nobel prize winners by the Common Council for American Unity, New York, December 10, 1942.

individual, the passive people. Sometimes that passivity is merely absorption in certain activities which the individual or the nation is unwilling to relinquish. Fate may be foreseen but unacknowledged.

So it was with this war. It was foreseen, it was feared, but we were engaged in activities which we did not wish to change. We did not want to discover the alternative. The result was the same as though we had been a passive people. Our fate came down upon us, and we wrestle with it today.

I wish it were possible for me to speak only gratefully now of military victories. The first half of the year 1942 was so barren of such victories that one must be grateful for good military news. But as Victor Hugo once put it, we are men and women of the mind and not of the sword. We must reflect upon what these victories mean, or may mean. That is, we cannot but ask ourselves how far victory must extend, if it is to be real victory.

I confess that, for myself, the war looms far larger today than it did a year ago. The shadow is not lessened, but lengthened and darkened. This war is growing graver and longer and more serious every day. Winston Churchill has said very truly that this war is not being fought all at once. He said, you will remember, that it would be won first in Europe and then if necessary elsewhere. He was speaking in terms of the sword alone, but it is equally true in terms of the mind. We know now what we could not know a year ago, that this war is not only between the United Nations and the Axis. We know that the war between the United Nations and the Axis is only the beginning of the real war, which remains the war between the principles of democracy

THE CHANGING WAR

and the principles of fascism. We know that in this the war has no geographical boundaries. We have said and it may be true that we are fighting a war to save civilization. But what we must foresee is that unless there is a miracle we will have to fight another war to save freedom. There was no miracle a year ago—there is no reason to hope for one now.

When did the character of this war change? I think we all entered into the war knowing that however it might have been avoided, it had to be fought with all the strength of body and will, since it was inconceivable that our enemies should prevail. It is even more inconceivable today that our enemies, Germany and Japan, should win. But the strange thing is that the shadow of war does not grow less as these enemies grow weaker. The heavy foreboding, which is upon the heart and mind of every thinking man and woman, is not lifted as it should be now, at the end of this incredible year. Why can we not take more comfort in today's news? It is comforting, yes. It is something to be grateful for that our military machine is better than the enemies' machine. Why, then, are we not comforted?

It is because we see a certain Fate coming closer to us, and these victories do not hold back its march. Somewhere in this year the step might have been taken which could have averted this Fate. Until that moment this war was being fought as a war for freedom. You remember how heartily all of our allies, in Asia as well as in Europe, entered into the war for freedom. No war that has ever been waged was entered into with more devotion to freedom than was this war. Millions of people, dark and light, rallied to the cause of democracy. I am not exaggerating when I say that there was a moment

WHAT AMERICA MEANS TO ME

when the great peoples of Asia were very close to the anti-Axis peoples of Europe and America. The love of freedom is deep in the hearts of those Asian peoples, deeper than it is in our own hearts, for they know as we do not, what it is to live for a hundred years without freedom. Could there have been a man great enough at that significant moment to have declared that this war was a war for the freedom of all peoples, we would not have had to face now, as we do face, another war of which this one is only the beginning. One can only hope at most, now, that there will be a breathing space between this war and the next. One cannot guarantee that there will be that space.

For we had no man great enough to declare at the necessary moment the true meaning of this war. Let us reckon with this fact—our leaders are men of local minds. They have not been able to think in terms of the world. And I mean by the world not merely the geographical world in military terms, so that an army is sent here or sent there. I mean the world of human beings. This war has been limited in its true aims. It has become a military struggle. It has ceased to be a fight for freedom.

The times do not always produce the man. When the peoples of Asia and of Africa, yes, and when many among our own peoples here and in South America, looked and listened and heard no great voice, at that moment the shadow of the long war ahead darkened and fell upon us. The peoples of Asia are further from us today than they have ever been. They are realizing soberly that they must find their salvation in themselves, and not with us. Allies we are, to a certain guarded degree for a moment, for a while, but they cannot trust us.

THE CHANGING WAR

They see that while this first stage of the war must be won against the Axis, there will be another war, following hard upon this one, a greater war, the real war for freedom, in which none yet sees clearly either friend or foe. It is not now so certain what this first war will gain us. Perhaps it will not even save civilization for us. For it is in wars that civilizations are lost, if they go on too long. Good ends are too often lost in the means.

The oppressed people of France, too, are not as close to us as they were. Military victory in Africa has not won us a victory among those in France who still love liberty.

Our own colored people are not closer to us at the end of this year than they were at the beginning. Military victory is not enough to lift their hearts.

Now it is quite true that this war is more than one war. There is a good deal of reason on the side of those who say let us fight one war at a time. For example, obviously in a purely military sense it is to our benefit if, in need of all possible allies, we can keep political France with us, even though the earth of France has been seized by the enemy. Obviously then the sensible thing is to sacrifice the faraway peoples of France's empire, and say nothing at this time about giving the hope of freedom to colonial peoples. Would political France fight so well on our side, when the moment comes, if she knew that there would be no empires at the end of this war? Would imperial Holland be so enthusiastic for the allied cause if her empire were no longer to exist if the United Nations won? There are many persons who argue that England herself would be less enthusiastic if her empire were not to be restored to her intact at the end of this war. One thing is true—the promise of freedom cannot be given to one colonial people without being given to all, and therefore it may be argued, prudently, that it is easier to make no promise of freedom. It is easier to cease talking about freedom at all. It is easier to say that we had better win the war before we discuss the postwar world. It is less disturbing to our allies, both actual and potential, three of whom are empires, with vast holdings in the East and in Africa.

So in this fashion, the war ceased to be a war for freedom and has become merely a war against the Axis. All of Asia now knows and acknowledges, and so must we if we are honest, that the principle of human equality and human freedom may have nothing to do with our victory in this war. Certainly the peoples of Asia are now coming to believe that for them our victory will have nothing to do with freedom and equality.

And who can give them any other hope? One hears everywhere of plans for a reconstructed Europe, of plans for feeding Europe's hungry millions, of health measures for Europe's sick and wounded. But who hears anywhere of feeding India's hungry millions, hungry not only in the brief years of this war, but always hungry? Eighty per cent of India's people do not know and have never known what it is to be adequately fed. Yet there are no plans made for feeding them. Medical care is even more inadequate in Asia, has always been, but who plans for that? There are no plans, there never were any plans. A medical watchguard is kept at the gates of the East in Egypt in the mid-east and at the western ports, lest the dread diseases of Asia creep into our countries, into the beloved Europe, but who has cared how many of the peoples of the East suffered and died? What plan was ever made for feeding the world that considered their hunger? What plan was ever made for the

THE CHANGING WAR

financial reconstruction even of India that gave the Indians any power of feeding or caring for themselves? None—none. And China has been left as alone.

The war has been limited still further. It is now not even a war to save civilization. It is only a war to save European civilization. For we of the West seem never able to realize that in the East there are civilizations far older and as great if not greater than Europe's civilization. Shall those not be saved? It was out of the Mid-east that Europe's civilization was once reborn. It will be out of the Far East, out of India and out of China, that our own civilization will be reborn. When we talk of saving only Europe we save a partial thing, a secondary thing. The civilization of Europe has never been an integrated, ordered civilization. Because of this, Europe has been the breeding place of wars, and will continue to be.

The roots of human civilization are in Asia, not in Europe. It is in Asia that people have learned the ways of living together that bring peace and not continual war. It is in Asia that people believe in and practice the laws of individual and collective freedom upon which alone peace can be built. The only war-like people there are the Japanese, whose civilization, like that of Europe, is derivative and secondary. But the millions of China and India and the South Seas have learned the principles of peace. They know that civilization is based upon peace, and only upon peace, and so they have valued peace above all else.

Let us face this moment in this year, therefore, and not be deceived in the nature of the struggle that lies ahead. None of us here is safe. Our kind anywhere is not safe. All the victories now being won do not make us safe. Those of us who are Jews are not safe, here or anywhere in the world. Those of us who are women are not safe here or anywhere else in the world. The determination to continue rule over colonial empires endangers us, the avowed will to maintain white supremacy at all costs in our own country endangers us. All those who belong to those testing places of democracy, the minorities, the Jews, the Negroes, the women, are endangered. All who are the agents of civilization, the intellectuals, the poets and artists and writers, the liberal in mind, the thinkers, the men and women of ideas, the idealists, are endangered. I am not afraid to speak to you boldly. The victory over the Axis does not mean the victory over fascism and you and I must know this, we must acknowledge it, we must reckon with it. Only thus can we do our part to save civilization—not only the civilization of Europe, of our own country, but human civilization, for all humanity.

What shall we do?

In the first place, we must refuse to be deceived by military victories. It is easy to be silenced when the noise of military trumpets fill the air. The clamor of hurrahs impels the unthinking to uncritical approval. But we are not the unthinking. It is our great sin when we yield ourselves, when we allow ourselves to be silenced, through fear or through hopelessness because our voices seem unheard.

You who have come to us from Europe, you must not be afraid to speak out, to help the rest of us to speak, when you see the emptiness of a merely military victory. I know how much you have endured and how deeply you long for a little peace now, how timid you feel in a country strange to you, where you are struggling again to establish yourselves. But you must not long for peace, for there is yet no peace anywhere. And no country is stranger to you than another. This country, our own dear land, may become strange to all of us, as Germany became strange to these who have come here as refugees, if we do not take our full part in this war. And our full part is to insist that the war is not won and cannot be won, unless democracy wins against fascism, here on our own soil, as well as in Europe, until people are free in Asia as well as in France.

Why have we been so silent these last months? When the war changed, when Asia was lost to us, as it is lost now, and is being more wholly lost with every day that passes—where were our voices? A few spoke, a few cried out. But these made only a little outcry. Where was the mighty outcry? It is our duty as citizens of democracy and as human beings not to be content today merely to put on a uniform, either the uniform of army or navy upon our bodies, or the uniform of docility upon our minds, or of expediency upon our hearts. Now as never before in the history of the world we who believe in liberty of the mind and freedom of the body must speak, again and again, regardless of the danger to ourselves. If we do not make this war into a war for freedom, we shall lose freedom, without which life is worthless. If freedom must be lost, then let us lose it boldly, still speaking what we know to be true and not in the timidity of silence. For us, words are weapons.

You will remember those days in the history of France, in the middle of the last century, when one of us, Victor Hugo, famous, wealthy, a friend of monarchs, came to see on which side righteousness was. He chose the side of the people, and it is for that choice that he must be remembered today. Because he and others like

WHAT AMERICA MEANS TO ME

him would not be silenced the life of France went on for almost a century longer. He lost, it is true, and the powers won, against which he fought so bravely, speaking when to speak was to defy death and accept exile. France has fallen now, perhaps more than anything else because those who might have replaced Victor Hugo chose to remain in prudent silence when they ought to have spoken. It was Victor Hugo who said what we must say today. He wrote in November, 1849, answering those who accused him of changing his party, "Last year I fought by your side because you defended civilization. This year I fight against you because you attack liberty." Of one who remained on the side of those who steadily developed the revolution toward dictatorship, he said, "He has passed to the side of those who oppress, but I remain on the side of those who are oppressed."

He fought on the side of the oppressed everywhere—wherever he found them: for the school teachers in villages oppressed by a narrow clergy, for working people who were oppressed by their employers. He fought against those who sought in every way they could to undermine the cause of democracy—democracy whose texture and soul are human equality and freedom, so that when these are denied in any degree in that degree democracy itself is denied.

We who belong in some measure, in one way or another, to that company of which Victor Hugo in his time was a master and a leader, let us at this moment, when the whole world is engaged in the struggle which in his day centered in France, determine our place as he did. Let who will pass over to the side of those who oppress, our place remains on the side of those who are oppressed.

10. NOT QUITE TOO LATE

EVERY great mistake has a halfway moment, a split second when it can be recalled and perhaps remedied. We are at that moment now in this war. It may be still possible to relate the past to the present, with hope of changing the future, by asking how have we failed, so far, in our war aims?

It is a difficult question to answer when we consider that these war aims have never yet been stated with authority except in the very general terms of the Four Freedoms. I do not include the Atlantic Charter, for Churchill early limited its application to Europe, and this is a global war. I do not include the statements of Vice-President Wallace, since he does not hold primary power, and since he has been so heartily contradicted both by action and lack of action. The only statement of global war aims, then, by any western leader, has been President Roosevelt's Four Freedoms. Promises of military action both in Europe and against Japan, such as those given by President Roosevelt and Mr. Churchill after the Casablanca conference, cannot properly be called war aims. It is a truism now to say that military

An article published substantially in this form in *The New York Times Magazine*, February 28, 1943.

WHAT AMERICA MEANS TO ME

victory in this war is only a necessary peliminary step toward a sound world peace.

The Four Freedoms, then, remain the sole statement yet given of our war aims.

But I take it that it is the constant and peacetime aim of any democratic government to make secure for its own citizens freedom of speech, freedom of religion, freedom from fear and freedom from want. If we are fighting for these freedoms "everywhere in the world," that is, for peoples who do not have them now, then we have to fight first for the basic freedom—*the freedom to be free*. It was an Indian, and the Indian was Gandhi, who pointed that out. And the only country to declare itself officially for the freedom of all peoples, and for equality among all, has been China.

Without this basic equality and freedom the other four freedoms cannot be secure.

For it is quite possible that even under a tyrant, if he were benevolent, the people would have the four freedoms. But the people must have a guarantee of their power against the tyrant who is not benevolent, and freedom is their only guarantee. This war is a war for that freedom, in which alone the four other freedoms can be realized. It was an Englishman, R. H. Tawney, who said, "Either war is a crusade or it is a crime. There is no halfway house." The crime in this war is that it has been kept from being a crusade.

We Americans have denied our own tradition of freedom in this global war. We had earlier made, it is true, an unequivocal declaration for freedom for the Philippines, and this served us well so far as it went. But when Burma fell, because China was not accepted as an equal ally, and when Cripps failed in his mission to India—

NOT QUITE TOO LATE

both events occurred in the same month, April, 1942—we Americans failed by our very silence. We acquiesced, by our silence, in the limitation of the aims of this war to freedom for some peoples, but not for others, to the four lesser freedoms, not freedom itself. Then and ever since we have evaded the true meaning of the war.

The people of China and India, and they are half the people in the world, are now forced to the conviction that we are fighting not for freedom as a principle of human life, but to maintain ourselves with the British in a position of superiority over them. To this conviction they have been compelled by three things; first, by our Anglo-American conduct of the war; second, by the open statements of Churchill's government; third, by our own silence. I say not only the peoples of China and India, but all the peoples of Asia, and I do not doubt of Africa, share in this conviction, and will shape their future action upon it if the conviction cannot be charged.

Let us review certain facts. Nine months before Japan attacked Singapore and the Netherlands Indies, Chiang Kai-shek declared that China was ready to help defend those islands and the South Seas. The offer was never accepted.

The day after Pearl Harbor was attacked, Chiang Kai-shek cabled to President Roosevelt pledging "all we are and all we have to the common cause against Japan." But we have not made common cause with China, even yet.

When Japan attacked Burma, Chiang Kai-shek demanded that China be allowed to help hold a region so essential to her own safety. The Chinese forces were not allowed to move into Burma at a time when they might have saved that country. Persons who were on the ground declared that the British were unwilling to have what they called "native" armies, fighting under their own officers, come among a subject people. The Chinese forces were held waiting for weeks on the border. By the time they were allowed to enter Burma, Rangoon had fallen and the allied forces were in irretrievable retreat. Three of China's best veteran divisions were cut to pieces, and one of their best generals killed, for they threw themselves into a battle already lost. They were left isolated again and again. The bridge over the Irrawaddy was destroyed by retreating British forces without notice to the Chinese, so that the Chinese were facing the Japanese alone.

The Imperial forces had no conception of what Burma meant to the war, because the aim of the war had never been declared and so made clear to them. They said, men and officers alike, and I have talked personally with those who heard them say it, "Why should we fight here? If we win the war Burma will be ours anyway. If we lose we'll lose Burma anyway." So they retreated. What they were too ignorant to know was that they were not fighting to hold Burma as a piece of the British Empire. They were fighting for the life line of China, the Burma Road, for the very soil of China, indeed, whence we ourselves could so easily and quickly have bombed Japan. Now Burma has to be retaken painfully, foot by foot. "War is either a crusade or it is a crime."

The Chinese have suffered more heavily from our failure in the aim of this war than any other nation. By the loss of Burma, China has been wellnigh wrecked. Why hide the truth? Our monthly output of planes is 5800. China has far fewer than one thousand planes. But when we could have sent planes to China we did not. We even allowed some planes destined for China to be held in India, and we allowed planes which had reached China to be taken away again and flown back to Egypt, just as we allowed planes destined for Russia to be diverted in Iceland. China is being choked off. Transport planes alone cannot possibly supply her with her share of war materials. The truth is that very little lend-lease material had actually gone over the Burma Road to China before the road was closed by the loss of Burma.

Instead of having Chinese representatives really sharing in our Anglo-American war councils, we kept them cooling their heels and their rightful anger upon the thresholds of Washington. The recent withdrawal of the Chinese military mission from our capitol has its deep significance in spite of official denials. One need only to listen to a group of Chinese talking among themselves to know how the confidence of the Chinese in us is passing. I do not mean to say that the Chinese do not trust us as human beings. The tolerant Chinese suppose we do the best we can. No, their confidence in us is being lost not because they think that we mean ill, but because they think that we do not know better. They expected more of us in the way of foresight, wisdom, and leadership.

They exalted our leaders beyond their worth. Because the Chinese, like other peoples of Asia, have always revered those whom they consider great men, they looked to us with eagerness for leadership not only military, but for a true leadership toward the thing for which they thought we all were fighting, the principle of freedom for all peoples. When Churchill repudiated this principle, and when Cripps failed, then all eyes were fixed upon us. But we were silent. That silence has cost us very dear, and if it is not broken and broken soon, it will cost us far more dearly yet and will cost our children very dearly indeed. Our unwillingness to declare the true aim of this war has not made that aim less clear to the peoples of Asia. For them it is still a war for freedom, and it will go on until it is won.

A determination for freedom in the world would, of course, cost us many of our prejudices. We could not assure freedom to the other peoples and keep our own Negroes in a position half slave, as they are now. It would cost us the prejudices which exclude the Chinese, for example, from immigrating into this country on a quota basis; that is, we would have to be willing to allow one hundred Chinese to come in legally each year.

It would cost us, too, the trouble of saying to England, "We really believe in the freedom of peoples, but we fully realize your dependence economically upon Empire, and so we are prepared to share with you the costs of setting your subject peoples free, in order that we may have a free world of cooperative peoples. We will help you to distribute the financial loss and to set up new enterprises which will pay you equally well. That is, we will share with you the responsibility of a real democracy for the world."

It would mean that we would have to pledge our word —and keep it—to the conquered peoples of Europe, including those in the Axis nations, that this time we will not withdraw and leave the mess to them while we demand our money back. It would mean that upon declaring our belief in the freedom of all peoples, we would put our shoulder to the job of making freedom workable.

NOT QUITE TOO LATE

But the avowed determination for democracy for all peoples is the only way to win this war for democracy. At least in the East our prestige has already suffered so greatly that I do not believe any military victory will restore it. For us it was a priceless prestige, more potentially valuable to us even than England's Empire to her. Our prestige was founded on something better than Empire—it was founded on the friendship and confidence of peoples who believed in us as those who stood for the principle of freedom for mankind. Upon us, now, has fallen the burden of the old misdeeds of empire, which we never deserved.

If we continue refusing to declare the true aim of this war, we shall have to reckon, when we carry the belated war into Asia, with peoples who have lost their eager enthusiastic belief in our greatness, and goodness. The peoples of India and Burma, of Malaya and the South Seas, will not forget our silence on the primary freedom —that of peoples to be free.

Even our close relations with England, for which we have sacrificed so much, are now marred by mutual distrust. In spite of sternly maintained silence in Washington, the American people trust England less because of what has happened and is happening in India. In spite of a less complete silence in Whitehall, the people of England trust us less because of our policy in North Africa: "a political cesspool," an English weekly puts it, "whose stench not merely infects the cause of the Western Allies but threatens, unless there be plain speaking and better understanding, to poison Anglo-American relations." Englishmen are telling us that Empire is the only recourse for them if we cannot assure them that isolationism will not again keep us from taking our share of the responsibility for world democracy. Isolationism walks hand in hand with imperialism to make victory for democracy impossible.

It is not only isolationism which is the enemy of our war aim, true democracy in the world. The determination to pursue individual lines of action and prejudice is still wrecking us. Our individual hates are still stronger today than our hatred of the enemy. There are Americans in the South who would rather see Hitler win than give up their discrimination against the Negro. There are other Americans who would rather lose the war than see equality granted to the Asian peoples. There are Englishmen who would rather let Hitler win than give freedom to India. These, too, are silent as to the real aim of the war.

Can this silence, maintained heretofore at such tremendous cost, be broken now? It can, but only by the people of the United States and England. Only the people can insist that the true aim of this war be stated. The peoples of Asia cannot understand why we, at least, will not say we believe in freedom as a principle applicable to all peoples. They reason that if we will not even say this, will we ever help to bring it about? Why should they believe we will?

What do they mean by freedom? For them as for all of us, freedom is the right to live and to govern one's own actions in accord with freedom for all, and they know, and we ought to know, that such freedom can only be maintained *for* all when it is maintained *by* all. Freedom for all peoples demands cooperation by all peoples. Freedom is compatible with and indeed dependent upon mutual cooperation in the world, in the same way as it is in any local community. Self-determination in individual persons or nations may result in gangsterdom and loss of freedom for everybody else. Where all are to be free, conditions must be maintained by all as a mutual responsibility. To declare that this war is for freedom, therefore, is to call for a form of world cooperation which alone can maintain that freedom—a cooperation of all peoples, who must first be free. Thus we would have begun at last the only sort of world in which war would no longer be inevitable. For so long as this world we now have goes on we shall have war after war. There is no promise yet that this war will be the last; on the contrary, other wars are already looming.

It is not yet quite too late to unite all peoples by the one thing which all peoples value above everything—not freedom only for religion, not freedom only of speech, not freedom only from fear or want—but the great freedom to be free. Here is the true aim of this war and until it is so recognized, until it is so declared, we will fail in achieving democracy. Men would rather be starving and free than fed in bonds. They would rather live in fear of all sorts of trouble and insecurity if they can only be free. We misjudge the highest nature of man when we think that if we can keep him fed and secure under his own roof, let him say what he likes and go to church on Sunday, then he will be content. He will not be content, anywhere in the world, until he lives a free man in a free country, his people free in a world of the free.

11. CAN THE CHURCH LEAD?

M Y FATHER was a minister in the Christian Church in a day when to be a minister meant to be a leader. I suppose he was a minister because he was by nature a leader and because he grew up in the Christian religion and so he combined religion and leadership. This combination led him to the foreign mission field, and for fifty years he was a leader of men in China. It was not a peaceful life for him or for his family, for to be a leader meant that though he had followers there were plenty who would not follow, and his life was an embattled one. But it was a successful life and when he died in his eightieth year—to his disgust, for he was planning new campaigns—he regretted none of it.

We who grew up as his children, therefore, were early accustomed to thinking of leadership as coming from the Church. In our community in China Christians were expected to take definite stands of leadership in all matters. If the members of my father's various churches scattered through the Chinese cities and towns in our region did not take such leadership he did not hesitate to inquire into the nature of their Christianity. For him the practice of religion was inseparable from its profession. In this tradition he reared us. It was a hard tradi-

First issued as a pamphlet by Mr. Harold A. Hatch.

CAN THE CHURCH LEAD?

tion if what one wanted was peace and comfort in daily life, but it made its mark upon its day.

I may be forgiven therefore if I came back to my own country expecting similar leadership from the Church here. That I did not find it except in isolated cases did not at first much disturb me. Times were changed, I thought. Moral leadership was perhaps to be found now in other places in our modern society. Or, I thought, it may be that the influence of the Christian is only more diffused in our society, so that it is not so much the Church corporate that works, as its representatives in secular life. We may have the Christian as groceryman, the Christian as teacher, the Christian as scientist, and so to all parts of life. This seemed to me valuable, for thus the twin pillars of the ideals of the Fatherhood of God and the Brotherhood of Man upon which the Church has always been founded could become the foundations, too, of our society.

Whether there has been this diffusion I do not know. But I do know that if there has been it is not strong enough for this hour of crisis. Individual Christians scattered through our life have obviously not influenced our society enough to be able now to take the leadership. They do not lead our people as Christian individuals. No, they have even come to be too much like those who do not profess the Fatherhood of God and the Brotherhood of Man. The Christian who in his community should be the first to take his stand upon those twin pillars of the Church denies them daily in his actions, even as do those whom he should lead. The Christian himself is not free from the prejudices which are most unchristian and insofar as he is not free, he cannot lead others. And yet the time has come when it is imperative

WHAT AMERICA MEANS TO ME

that moral leadership be found somewhere in our nation if we are to win the war and insure the peace after three centuries of failure.

For today it is obvious that although we are increasingly in earnest about this war, we are not yet putting forth our full effort to win it. This is not through lack of wish to win, but through lack of will to win. Every true American knows that we must win, lest we lose that for which our nation was founded. Intellectually this is accepted by all who believe in American democracy. If energy could spring from intellectual conviction our war efforts, individual and national, would swing into full and unified production, and those who do not believe in democracy would soon find themselves defined and on the wrong side. But energy does not spring out of intellectual conviction. Its source is deeper in the human frame. Intellectual conviction may be the spark which lights the tinder which supplies the energy, but it is no more than that. The will to act finally comes out of the heart, not the head.

Why is it that as yet this will has not been stirred in our people? We are going through all the proper motions for war, but the all-out determination to win has not yet taken hold of us. The cause for this spiritual apathy is simple—there are emotions stronger in us than the will to win this war for freedom and human equality. For, basically, this is of course what the war is about, and the reason we are not yet generating full energy is that we know it is what the war is about but we do not want and are not willing to allow our knowledge to pass over into the seat of energy in us, because of conflicting emotions there. That is, we cannot fight to win a war for freedom so long as practically we do not want freedom for all peoples, and we cannot fight to win a war for human equality if we do not actually want human equality. Bluntly, the man or woman who is determined to keep alive the traditions of empire in Asia or Africa is putting imperialism ahead of winning the war, and the man or woman who insists on Jim Crowism and total Oriental exclusion at home is putting race prejudice ahead of winning the war. And if these two are to be the pillars of our society instead of the Fatherhood of God and the Brotherhod of Man, we had better know it and stop wasting our people in this war for freedom and human equality. We cannot possibly win it.

Here then is the spiritual confusion in which Americans now are and out of which we must somehow be led. We are faced with the necessity of fighting a war for principles in which we say we believe but which actually we do not want to practice. We talk about the American way of life and we go on tolerating and encouraging and demanding Jim Crowism and Oriental exclusion which are the Nazi way of life. We can never get pure energy out of such a conflict. The spark is applied to wet tinder. There will be no flame.

The truth is that we have not yet carried the war into the places where it really hurts. We can give up sugar, but we cannot give up segregation. We are willing to ration our gasoline but we do not want to insist that colored labor shall have equal rights with white labor. We consent to the heaviest of taxes for military warfare but we are not willing to treat the Chinese as we treat the British. We are ready, that is, to give up anything material, but nothing else. Unfortunately democracy cannot be bought with material goods, nor is human equality to be paid for with silver. Democracy can only be won by the sacrifice of everything that is undemocratic, and human equality can only be had by the will to have it at all costs.

The material sacrifice is easy, the spiritual sacrifice is hard, and it is here that our people must be led. For the easy material sacrifice is not enough and the hard spiritual sacrifice must be made before our full energy is behind this war. Where shall we get the strength to dig into our own secret places and root out the enemy within ourselves? Where are our moral leaders? Now if ever the Church must provide them, both for its own sake and for the sake of our people. For if the Church cannot at this moment see the issue clearly and simply enough to lead the people to the realization of its age-old belief in the Fatherhood of God, by proclaiming its determination to practice the Brotherhood of Man through the refusal any longer to condone imperialism and race prejudice, then the Church is dead, and from that death there is no resurrection. Never, I think, in history, have human issues been as clear as they are today when millions of people in our own country and in all parts of the world cry out for one thing—freedom. And the only way to establish freedom as a way of life upon the earth is to determine that men are indeed brothers, and that all shall be treated alike, without regard to color or class. Where is the Church that it does not come forward and declare itself not only as a body corporate, but through its own members in the separate practice of their individual lives?

Nor can the Church delay. Before our eyes this war for democracy may turn into a war for new empire. It is high time that we realize our own danger. For it is a danger when there are Americans who are not willing

CAN THE CHURCH LEAD?

to declare openly the principle of human equality and are not willing to practice the principle. We have here in our own country the strongest possible elements of danger to democracy, and there is little time left in which to recognize them and to stay their increasing power. Those who say that we are not fighting for anything except our American way of life—are they better than those who fight for any other way of life, if both those ways of life include the subjection of peoples to their rule? Will not such a way of life in America lead simply to more war as it has everywhere else in the world? Is our way of life to be immune from evil consequences if it contains within itself the same seeds of prejudice and greed and selfishness that have made all treaties of peace fail in the last three centuries? It is folly to think that we can escape.

And can we hope to escape fascism itself in this country if there are those here speaking openly and loudly the very dogmas that brought about the fascist regime in Germany? Those dogmas are: first, race prejudice on a basis even broader here than the race prejudice in Germany; second, impatience with the slow methods of democratic processes; third, greed in business and labor; and fourth, the baiting of all those who question race prejudice and intolerance and greed. The beginning of fascism has always been the attempt to suppress intelligent inquiry and the moment this suppression is successful, intellectuals are put into prison and killed and the books are burned. Can it happen here? It can happen here, in the name of communism or fascism or lack of patriotism or by any other name.

Yet there are many who wait for leadership toward true democracy. All over our country there are the young, ready to be led out of old prejudices and dead traditions. The young are ready to believe in human equality. Even in the South there are young white people, men and women, who say, "We are ready to treat the colored young people as our friends and equals—it is the older people who are clinging to traditions." There are others, good people who have not the strength to stand alone in their goodness. They are confused and they must be led out of their confusion to know that the basic issues in this war are simple and within the mental comprehension of all. Whether they are within the practical application of all depends upon the strength of our determination now not to repeat the mistakes of the centuries, and for that determination we need moral leadership. Millions in Asia and Europe and Africa, too, wait for the leadership in this war which will declare itself for freedom and human equality for all. If we cannot find that leadership then this war will end again in futile peace.

For during the last three hundred years there have been ten treaties made in Europe alone, all calling for a "Christian peace"—that is, a peace based on human brotherhood. Yet not one of them has produced this "Christian peace," from the Treaty of Westphalia to the Treaty of Versailles. They have been intellectual treaties, and the men who made them paid lip service to the idea of human equality. Even President Wilson was not willing to include racial equality in the Treaty of Versailles. Yet any treaty which is not based upon human equality and implemented on human equality will bring the world no peace. Treaties therefore have been nothing but intellectual agreements, and they have been denied and made useless by the prejudices of those who

CAN THE CHURCH LEAD?

would not observe them. And who can observe any treaty for peace who is not willing to give up his own personal prejudices as part of the necessary sacrifice? And if we have not the moral energy to make this sacrifice even to win the war how can we hope to win the peace?

Now, if ever, the Church ought to furnish the leadership for our people to make the sacrifice of our prejudices and our greed which through all the centuries we have not been strong enough to make. If the Church cannot produce the necessary moral leadership then religion is dead indeed. It may be that religion is dead, and if it is, we had better know it and set ourselves to try to discover other sources of moral strength before it is too late.

But how is it that the Church today does not recognize even its own danger? The only hope of freedom for religion is in the freedom of all mankind. Does the Church in our country think it will escape the fate of the Church in the fascist countries if it does not now take the moral leadership necessary for its own life as well as the life of the nation? Yes, perhaps it is true that religion is already dead and what we have is nothing but the shell of what might have been alive and is no more.

And yet, I am loath to believe that the Church is really dead. For I know the Church is no separate entity in itself. It is only men and women of a certain mind and temper and spirit, who declare in themselves their belief in the Fatherhood of God and the Brotherhood of Man. But perhaps they believe only intellectually and not in their hearts and so they sleep. If they are only sleeping, then let them awake. If the Church in our country does not lead now, it may never have the opportunity again. Now is the moment of crisis.

How shall we awaken this sleeping Church? Alas, I know no other way except the way by which men and women are awakened anywhere. Will men and women of the Church practice what they profess? Those who say they believe in the Brotherhood of Man, will they act as they believe? Can the Church rise to this new greatness? But so to rise again means that within the Church itself there must be the determination to sacrifice everything which stands in the way of such greatness—that is, individual men and women who are the Church must be willing to sacrifice their own prejudices first before they can become the leaders of others for freedom and human equality.

Is there this life in the Church? I do not know. But if there is not, then indeed we must look elsewhere for the light.

12. CHILDREN AND THE WORLD

I.

CHINA is full of children. They are gay, round, laughing little people, their black hair braided into tight tails with red cord, their black eyes sparkling and full of mischief. In summer time they run around with nothing on, or very little, and in winter they are bundled into padded garments which make them into toddling puff balls. Many a time I have seen a round mite just able to walk, who being in his winter garb could not get up when he fell down, and had to lie kicking futilely until someone passing set him right side up. A flash of a smile, a giggle, and off he went again.

China's children have the look of the children of the free. There is no cringing in those frank black eyes. They are well loved children and they know it. How well loved they are! To heal a sick child, to feed a starving one, is to win the eternal friendship of the Chinese who, as a people, adore children. Thus it certainly was

The first section of this chapter appeared in *Harper's Bazaar*, April, 1942. The second section is part of a speech for the Save the Children Association in New York, January 27, 1943. The third section is part of a speech for the Civilian Defense Volunteer Office in New York, March 18, 1943.

in the case of Siao Fah, a little Chinese boy born in my own house.

Siao Fah's mother was a poor woman whom I was not particularly glad to see one day when she turned up at my door, alone, pregnant, and starving. She had walked hundreds of miles from a northern town where I had once lived and where there was now a famine. I did not even know her except as the wife of a rather worthless gardener who at last had had to be discharged. But here she was, and of course she could not be turned away. She stayed, very quiet and humble, eating her way back to health. When the time came for her baby to be born she insisted, after the way of her village, that she wanted no one with her. Nothing could make her change her mind, and so I prepared sterile tools and gave her a bottle of iodine for disinfectant, and much advice besides. She had lost all her other babies at birth, from tetanus.

Three hours later she called to me to come and see her son. That was the first time I saw Siao Fah. He lay in a cradle that my own children had used, and was undoubtedly the cutest baby I had ever seen. Of course I know babies cannot smile as soon as they are born, but I swear that when he looked at me, as he did, a smile was already in his eyes.

He grew like a dark rose, for a day, and then suddenly I woke up one midnight at the sound of his mother's weeping. "My son is about to die!" she wailed.

I ran into the room where she was, and saw at once that indeed Siao Fah was about to die. I stripped off his little garments and there on his tiny belly was a horrible festering sore. The poor mother, believing in the goodness of iodine, had poured the whole bottle on his navel.

Siao Fah and I fought a battle with death for a week.

CHILDREN AND THE WORLD

We had to fight it alone because there was no doctor in the city. Several times I thought Siao Fah was going to give up but I would not let him. I kept him with me day and night until I saw he was going to pull through. He did, and again the dark rose went on growing.

At three months he was perfect. Every day I inspected him. His little mouth was red, his cheeks red, and his eyes lamps of joy. His mother made him a red silk coat, and shaved his head except for a pigtail in the middle.

Then one day his father turned up and that meant a home had to be started. It was made in a little rented house of earth just over the compound wall, and it was a happy home, all centered around Siao Fah.

But once again Siao Fah and I had a battle to fight with death. One spring morning his mother came running through the gate with him in her arms. I knew it was she because I heard the familiar wail of death. Yes, there she was, and once more Siao Fah was dying. He had been burned accidentally.

So we fought the war against death again, and this time I was not patient. I told Siao Fah's mother bluntly that she was not fit to have Siao Fah, and she agreed with streaming tears. It was a longer fight this time, and I was hopeless from the start. But Siao Fah came of a tenacious stock, and he had a hold on life. Again he pulled through.

By the time he was a year old he was a child whom the gods envied. When his mother brought him to see me he always wanted to see the roses, and there he would stand among them, pulling off rose leaves and laughing, and his mother and I looked at him and laughed, too.

Who would have thought that Siao Fah would in

effect one day save my own life? And yet so it was to be.

There came one of those revolutionary turns in a China then troubled and disunited, when a mob took over the city briefly and some white men lost their lives, and all stood in danger. In that desperate day it was Siao Fah's mother who came running into the compound and gathered us all together, I and my children, and led us to her little hidden lowly house and kept us safe there through forty-eight hours of horror. Again and again she defended us against those who were afraid they might be killed, too, if we were found there.

"I will say it is all my fault if they are found here," I heard her arguing over and over with her landlord.

Well, we were not found and we were rescued at last, and as we were taken to safety again, I gave Siao Fah a great hug. He was holding his mother's hand as we passed.

"Aren't you coming back, foster mother?" he asked me, beginning to cry. He could talk then.

"Certainly I am coming back," I said.

I did come back and Siao Fah had many a merry afternoon with my own children.

Where is Siao Fah now? The last time I heard from him his mother did not know. The Japanese had taken over the city. She cannot write, for Siao Fah did the writing. But she found a friend to write for her—"Our son is with the hill men," she wrote me. Siao Fah had escaped and joined the guerrillas!

I am sure he is not dead. I remember too well the will to live that I saw in the two battles we fought together against death. No, he is alive somewhere in the hills, a sturdy lad of eighteen now, waging the long war for freedom.

CHILDREN AND THE WORLD

II.

I suppose there has never been an age when children have suffered more heavily than they have in this one. It is ironical that in an age when we have prided ourselves on our progress in the intelligent care and teaching of children we have at the same time put them at the mercy of new and most terrible weapons of destruction. Men and women have a voice in the management of the world's affairs whether they use their voices or not, but little children have no voice. They can only share in complete bewilderment the horrors of this age—heroes and martyrs in their childish ways, but always helpless and bewildered.

When I contemplate the mass misery of children in the world today I confess it far overtops in my own mind anything which soldiers suffer or even civilians. Civilians have of course suffered a great deal more than soldiers in this war, and this is true in every country. The civilians of China have suffered on a scale infinitely worse than soldiers have—the millions dead are unknown. It is roughly estimated that fifty million people have been driven out of their homes. Untold millions have died from disease and deprivation and starvation and among those are millions of children. Children have suffered in Europe even though on a lesser scale, and in England they have suffered not only from death but from loss of home and security. In our own country I sometimes think it is only our children who have really suffered any shock from the war. That they do suffer can easily be seen from the news of their delinquencies and disturbances.

But it must be taken into consideration that even

when there was no war there were great areas of the earth where the brunt of deprivation fell and continues to fall upon children. I think no one can travel in India even superficially without realizing that the degrading poverty which is almost universal in India falls most heavily upon India's children. More than one generation of India now has grown up through a half-starved, anxious, insecure childhood, and that explains more in India today than is commonly known or than many people care to believe.

Lest we be too complacent, let us remember our own children. I was talking with Sigrid Undset a few weeks ago and she told me she had just returned from a trip to Florida. Then she said, "I was shocked by the children I saw in the South. For misery and filth and lack of care they were worse than anything I have ever seen in Europe." I have seen some of those children, the children of sharecroppers and tenant farmers, both colored and white, and I never saw anything more tragic even among the poor of China. In China when the children are miserable, it is usually because of famine or catastrophe. Here in our rich country it is neglect, if not the parents' neglect, then our neglect. We do not have famines and there is no catastrophe which we cannot control. The condition of children in the poor South—or for that matter in sections of such places as Harlem—is due not to a catastrophe or to famine but to our indifference to their welfare.

And yet in these last months I have come to feel, rightly or wrongly, that there is something worse for all these little children than death. Worse than death will be to grow up in a world such as we now have, where war can fall at any moment upon innocent and ignorant peoples, and war that is more cruel with every succeeding out-break. I see no particular use in saving children alive for recurrent war to catch them later. I see no use in the enormous waste of women's lives in going on even to produce children when they are to be at the mercy of inhumanity and greed for power and race hatred. There is no reality in saving the children merely by giving them food and shelter. Somehow the saving has to go further than this. While we feed them and shelter them we have to do more for them—we have to develop them somehow into men and women who will not be at the mercy of such misery again. We have to save not only their bodies, but their minds and their hearts, or else the bodies are better lost.

I have come to the place of feeling that mere relief, if not accompanied by more than physical relief, is not worth giving any more. If a dollar given for food cannot carry more than a dollar's worth of food, I will put my dollar somewhere else. Something has to be done now not only to save the bodies of people from physical death but the minds from growing into the minds of those who will carry on the sort of world we have now—and those who silently endure are just as much those who carry on this sort of world as those who actively force it upon us. Rebecca West in that great book, *Black Lamb and Grey Falcon,* analyzed with genius the causes for the hotbed of quarrels in the Balkans which have led to so many wars. She makes it very clear that it is not only the Grey Falcons, the active aggressors, who are responsible for the barbarous times into which we have fallen; the Black Lambs are just as responsible, the silent sufferers, the ones who endure meekly and by their very meekness invoke and encourage the aggressors.

WHAT AMERICA MEANS TO ME

Let us consider the world of children at this moment, the world we must save. In our country there are children growing up in circumstances which cannot produce a peaceful world.

Think of the moment which faces every colored mother and father, the moment when their child has to know that he is doomed to eternal handicaps because of his color! There is not a single colored parent, unless he is imbecile, who does not dread that moment, who is not saddened by it and degraded by it. I know, for I have heard them talking about it, dreading it before it came, sorrowful after it had come. Imagine it for yourselves—how could you explain it to the child? How could you excuse yourself that you ever gave him birth? There are still other groups here, Jews, Poles, Hungarians and others, differing in different sections of our country where prejudice against so-called "foreigners" varies; but these can often escape at least by moving away from the region of prejudice. There is no escape for the colored child. He is born black if he has a drop of colored blood in him. Can these children be saved?

In India millions of little children are born subject. I don't think they suffer as acutely from it as our own colored children suffer here, for the Indian children live in a country where the white man, though his power is absolute, does not come into daily touch with the children. And yet anyone who has lived at all in India knows how the shadow of subjection is over everyone, and the children all know and live in that shadow. Can these children be saved?

The children of Europe will never escape wholly from the influence of what they have endured in these last years. We have to reckon with a crippled generation, and of course I do not mean only physical cripples. These children can never be wholly saved, yet I say quite frankly that I do not feel as sorry for them as I do for our own colored children, who are born under the shadow generation after generation, and cannot hope for escape even for their children. Yet somehow the children of Europe must be saved in so far as they can be saved, and not only for their own sakes, but because there have to be created in Europe peoples with whom the rest of us can live and work in some sort of cooperation.

I feel that no relief is better than a partial relief which saves only a child's body alive. It is better for the world if children die than if they are merely kept alive. You will say that children do recover if they are sheltered, fed, and made to feel secure again. And I say what is the use of their recovering at all if it is only to continue in a world where nothing real is yet being done to *save children?* Giving a child physical care is the merest beginning.

To save children, we must take active part in working for the removal of race discrimination, because children cannot be saved from the evil effects of race discrimination. War is only part of those effects—the peacetime ills are almost as severe and certainly more prolonged. The next war will come out of race discrimination unless something is done soon to prevent it.

To save children we must take active part in working for the elimination of war and the discovery and control of the war-like men who ride to power in times of social and economic disturbance. Race prejudice and war are the two greatest causes of suffering to children.

To save children we must take active part in all groups working for economic security for all people, for next to race prejudice and next to war, poverty brings the greatest suffering upon the world's children.

And in these days everything has to be thought of in terms of the world. It is meaningless to feed France's children if we do not feed our own sharecroppers' children. It is useless to feed Europe's children or our own unless we feed the children of Asia. There will be no peace if part of the world's children grow up disabled.

Our work is only just begun.

III.

There are two ways of being interested in children. One is the interest natural to us all in our own children primarily. This may be extended to the children of our community or of our race or of our own country. Most people have this interest to some extent. Then there are those fools, of whom I am one, who love any child, for some obscure reason or no reason at all. It is an inexplicable love, for a child is a human being and may be very unpleasant as a human being. A child may be ugly and carry his evil inheritance obviously in face and manner and intellect, and yet there are some of us who love such children and all children, who excuse everything to a child and see in children the hope of life and the reason why life continues to be worth while. I am one of those. Black and white and yellow and mixed, they are all the same to me, and no roof is large enough to shelter all the ones I would like to have under it. I trust this lack of discrimination will not invalidate what I say.

I cannot think only of our own children here in New York or in America. My mind goes all over the world, seeing children in China and children in Russia, children in Africa and India, yes and in Japan and Germany, too, where the children at least are still innocent. What is the world doing to them all now and what will they do to the future?

War has its heaviest impact upon children. They are the least prepared for it. They do not read the news or if they do read it is with childish lack of understanding. They only see that grown people are behaving in fearful inexplicable ways—killing each other. A bomb falling out of the sky is horrible enough to anyone, but to a child it is monstrous, a catastrophic nature falling upon him. He is atomic enough anyway, his whole struggle at the best of times being to realize himself as an independent being and to stabilize himself in some sort of security. In a world such as we have today it is impossible for a child to get beyond being an atom, and impossible for him to feel security without help of the most special kind. What kind of help can we give him?

It is the sort of help which we need for ourselves, all of us, adults as well as children. We need security. We have to find security ourselves before we give it to our children, we have to recognize and believe in our own beings and in the value of ourselves as individuals before we can help the child to believe in his.

Security for the child has, of course, been simply ripped out of the world. We built that security on material things, on the four walls of a home, on a community and established community life, on church and schedule and a settled government. Those are all fine things but they were never secure, really, at any time, had we understood our world. The only kind of a world in which security could be built on such things would have been a world in which all peoples were cooperating in maintaining a mutual security. Until and unless we are ready to do our share in a cooperative world society it will simply never again be safe to let a child grow up thinking that home or home town or home country offers any kind of security to him. They do not. An aggressive neighbor can at will bomb any of us at any time. This war has been so far all that it was foretold it would be. The next one will be worse. We hear it said often that the era immediately after the war will make airplanes as universal as cars were before the war. Huge improved airliners will make a week's vacation into a world tour. It takes any sensible child no time at all to realize that such progress in airships can mean also super-bombers which would bomb around the world as easily as fly on a pleasure tour.

The old security of home and community is gone, never to return. We have to build a deeper security than that for our children, a security founded not upon material things.

What will this security be? It must be simply a new affirmation of the value of the human individual. Until the single individual, who is any human being, is worth something again we shall not have a secure world. Fascism is not to be blamed entirely for this loss of value of the individual. Indeed in a curious perverted way fascism is the assertion of an individual, the monstrous individual asserting himself over others at whatever cost. Fascism may, could we penetrate deeply enough into its dark sources, be the result of the reaction of strong individuals, wrongly taught, reacting against the facelessness of the modern man, a facelessness for which a certain kind of limited science has been as responsible as anything else, the perversions of science, which have reduced

CHILDREN AND THE WORLD

the spirit of man to nothing, and have called man nothing but a handful of chemicals, forgetting therefore even to be scientific. For who understands the power of the forces generated even by the mixture of chemicals? It is not the handful of chemicals of which our blood and bones and flesh are made that is ourselves. We are the force, the spirit, created from the interplay between chemicals. But the chemicals are only means for the creation and then only the cellular vessels containing the force which is our true being, that force which men call spirit and men call soul, but which is the uncomprehended, real self of any human creature. And the magic of this mixture of chemicals, and again it is a magic which no scientist has ever understood, is that the mixture is never quite the same, and so the force which it creates is never quite the same, and so every human being is different from every other human being, scientifically different as well as spiritually different. In this eternal difference there is the soundest basis for man's individuality. We are not faceless, we human beings. However they regiment us with uniforms, we are individuals. In the recognition of the individual soul alone can security be found for our children.

Therefore I would emphasize at every point the individuality of the child and the value of children's differences and the interest to be found in those differences. Teach the child to feel that individual differences are good and valuable. Contradict as deeply and as far as possible those attitudes which an insular society accustomed to material security has built up, that those of a particular kind are better than those of another. Break up the notion that security is to be found in a certain race and in a certain class. It is false to the truth indeed to allow children to believe that such things as class or color can protect them any more than houses can, or cities or states or distance.

By what fearful tragedies have we not been taught that there is no more security in being white, in being well-to-do, in being English or American instead of African or Burmese! My mind goes back to a story I heard from a young Chinese girl. She was in Hong Kong when the Japanese took that city. She said that the most tragic aspect of that most tragic fall was the total unpreparedness of the English and Americans who had lived in Hong Kong so many years as a superior group that they could not believe that the things which had made them secure for so many years—their color, their wealth —were simply no use any more—were, indeed, hazards instead of protections.

"I wondered," she said, "and my heart ached while I wondered, at the pretty English and American women in the hotels and the night clubs. The Japanese were a few miles away, but they sat there with their hair so beautifully waved, their cheeks pink and their lips rouged, in their lovely dresses. And I thought, 'How great is their danger!' And yet they could feel no danger, could see no danger, in spite of knowing what had happened to Chinese women. They could not believe it would happen to them."

And yet, in a few days, it happened to them. The Japanese came in and the English and Americans stayed in their beautiful homes on the Peak. The Japanese sent out orders that all were to come down to the waterfront. They did not come—they could neither read nor understand Japanese. But neither could they understand that Japanese could order them as though they were con-

CHILDREN AND THE WORLD

quered Chinese. The Japanese ordered again, and again they did not know enough to come. Some of them in their ignorance began to think everything was going to be all right because they were white and they were rich. The second command had said that all those who did not obey immediately would be punished. The punishment was this—the Japanese went up the Peak and bayonetted all the white people they saw and could find except the girls and young women. The girls between thirteen and twenty were given to the Japanese officers, because, as the young Chinese girl told me, "they were sure to be free from disease." The women over twenty were given to the common soldiers.

In a world like this, what security can we give our children except the security of belief in the value of the individual human soul, whatever his color and kind?

You may ask, what use is it to teach this? Is this a security in the face of what is happening around us? I see no other security except the stern insistence on the value of the human being. Only in such teaching, inexorable even in the face of hideous denials, is there any hope of the return of the spirit of humanity to the earth again. This war is an explosion of brutality, the fruit of a long education in dehumanization. We have allowed science to dehumanize us. We have allowed science to disintegrate us, to reduce us to a handful of chemicals, and the spirit of man in despair has turned upon man. We have insisted that we were animals and we have become animals, rending one another like beasts. None of us will be safe until we realize that only in restoring the spirit of humanity, that is, by recognizing man's individual soul, can we be safe.

We must change the whole basis of our education.

WHAT AMERICA MEANS TO ME

Instead of the emphasis on the material we must emphasize the human. Chemicals are not to be called important because men and women can be reduced to chemicals. Chemicals are only important because put together in a certain magic way these chemicals make a man and a woman, living creatures, thinking, moving, breathing, loving, feeling. So with every material element. All are important only in so far as they serve man's spirit, not his flesh. They are important to the flesh only when they serve the spirit that dwells in the flesh.

The security, then, which we must somehow give our children is not the security of house and garden, of home and community, of all the settled ways of peace. It is not safe to let them believe in such security, for it no longer exists. But there is a security deeper and bottom true. It is the security of the soul taught to believe in the worth of mankind, to the last individual, and so in its own worth.

But we would not be establishing this security if we did not at the same time teach our children that there is an enemy in the world, and the enemy is the belief which opposes this, the belief, born of a limited understanding of the true dimensions of our universe and of man's being, that man is worthless and that he is fit only for the material of systems. Those who believe this are under the power of their belief and become part of it, and not in themselves as men but because they are part of an evil thing they must be considered the enemy.

No child today ought to be brought up thinking that peace is ahead. To let a child believe that this war may end any day and the world go back to something that was, is to deceive him so deeply that he will be wrecked by the reality of the future, and not only wrecked by it,

CHILDREN AND THE WORLD

but because he is wrecked unable to make that future into what it can be and ought to be, a victory for mankind.

For we have this double duty toward our children, not only to prepare them for the future, but to make them understand that *they are the future*. Upon them, upon the quality of their spirits, depends the kind of world we shall all have. If they grow up as the last generation grew up, shrinking from the horrors of the first world war, seeking relief and retreat when there could be no relief and retreat, we shall have other wars which our side will lose—our side that believes in the freedom of man and the worth of the individual.

This war will not be won when Hitler is vanquished. The enemy lives in a hundred places, in every country. It lives in the hordes of the Japanese, but it lives elsewhere, too. We have to train our children for a long war —perhaps for physical war, but certainly for a long war of the spirit.

Let us then tell our children frankly, "You will not have a peaceful life. You will be called upon again and again to decide great questions of right and wrong. Sometimes you will have to fight for what you believe is right. Therefore it is very necessary that you are clear in your own mind on what is right. We on our side believe that people should be free, and that in order that all may be free we must learn how to live so that all can be free, and not just one or two at the expense of the others."

With this goal in mind every incident of every day should lead toward it. Questions at home and school should be decided in the light of the future. It is a process of toughening, but not the sort of false physical thing that we have called toughening. Our boys and girls ought to know that the bully type, the false "tough," has been the first to break down under the actual fire of battle. The quiet, the calm, the determined have made the best soldiers. Why? Obviously the bully is insecure in himself—he blusters to muster his own courage. Children ought to know that. They ought to be taught to retort to the bully, "You're a coward or you wouldn't make such a noise about being brave. The really brave man simply acts brave—he doesn't have to talk about it." Put the iron into their souls, if the future is to be saved, for them as well as for all mankind.

Is it too hard for the child? Will their souls be seared? No—their souls will grow and blossom. There is nothing that the individual so fears as that he is in himself small and of no worth. We see the extremes of this fear in men like Hitler—we see it affect a whole nation of people like the Japanese. Give the individual the belief in himself which assures him in the first place that he is of infinite worth because all men are of worth, and in the second place assures his worth because of a great work he has to do, a war to be won for the worth of his own being, and you give him at once a security which nothing can destroy, a power which strengthens the feeblest of human beings.

All humanity is longing today to believe that mankind is of worth. The peoples of the world are rising up to ask. "Are we not men, are we not women?" Humanity is in protest against the enemy, wherever he is found, who would deny to men and women their infinite individual worth, who would reduce them to a handful of ashes, to dry chemical dust. We *are* men, we *are* women, we ought to believe in our worth, for it is true that we

CHILDREN AND THE WORLD

are force and power, spirit and mind and soul, born of a compound which none of us can understand. We call it creation. We are created, we know no more how, today with all our knowledge, than we did in the days when we knew nothing. We are created not as men make machines by mass production, but created each separate and individual to himself, and so each with his peculiar worth because he is separate and individual. When we fight for our own separate and individual worth we fight for all.

Here is the security our children need and all they need. Safe in that security, in them the future of mankind is safe.

13. TO WIN THE PEACE

THE twenty-sixth of January is celebrated as the anniversary of India's declaration of independence. On January 26, 1930, great gatherings everywhere in India peacefully and solemnly, as Nehru said, took the pledge of independence, without any speeches or exhortation. This day is still a day of faith, for the evidence of the thing hoped for is not yet seen.

The events of the past year have been important not for what they have accomplished for freedom, but for what they have not accomplished. They have shown us where we are in the world. They have shown what this war is and what it is not.

It is a good thing to know where we are. Confusion is the chief enemy of progress. Those who love freedom and who believe in human equality need not now be confused any more. It is not pessimism, I think, to know where one is, even if to know is to discover that one is not where one hoped to be. *To know* is the first necessity, to accept that knowledge without discouragement and to use it as a basis for further action is the second necessity, to believe in final achievement is the third necessity. These three necessities we have and we are not

A speech delivered at a meeting in New York to celebrate India's Independence Day, January 26, 1943.

dismayed. The war for the freedom of peoples in a world cooperation will be far longer than this war, the suffering for the world will be still more intense. But the end is no less sure.

We all know now that India will not be given her freedom by the present existing power. Sir Norman Angell clarified the new British position in a long letter to *The New York Times* on January 17. Britain will not and cannot change her imperial policies and government because, as he says, she fears American isolationism and until and unless she can be sure of American support in a changing world the Empire will stand as it is. Thus we find that it is America that is responsible for the fact that India is not to have her freedom. If it is so, let us accept the blame.

But Sir Norman claims perhaps a little too much for the British Empire when he goes on to say it is the one sound organization in a degenerating world. It is not quite true that the British Empire alone has held back the forces of the Axis. Russia and China have borne the brunt of the war, and they are no part of the British Empire. We must remember, too, that large parts of the British Empire have not held but have gone over to the enemy.

Sir Norman says in his new book, *Let the People Know*, "As to India, Burma, Africa and other Asiatic and colored countries, self-government has difficulties that do not present themselves in the case of a country like Canada or Australia."

These difficulties, it appears, are that India, Burma, Africa, and other Asiatic and colored peoples cannot be advanced to self-government as has been done with Canada, New Zealand and Australia, which are offshoots of the English people. But Sir Norman says that as soon as England is perfectly certain of the unshakeable and eternal support of India, Burma, Africa and other Asiatic and colored peoples for the people of England, assured of their support in peace and in war, those peoples may hope for freedom, too, within the British Empire. Or as Lady Astor aptly put it in regard to China and Russia, "I would like China and Russia to be in the framework of a new society formed by America and the British Commonwealth, but they would have to get into the 'British way of thinking.'" Until India, Burma, Africa and other Asiatic and colored peoples, can "get into the British way of thinking," they cannot expect freedom even within the British Empire. It would be folly not to reckon with this fact.

Since it appears that Britain's reluctance to give up her imperial policies and government is because American isolationism will not help her to maintain a world order if she does, let us ask how entrenched is isolationism in this country? Can India and Burma and Africa and all other Asiatic and colored peoples count on us to abandon isolationism and support, not the British Empire necessarily, but the job of taking a full share in world cooperation? The British are perfectly right in saying that we must give evidence of being willing to do our share at least, and that if we do not give this evidence, they can only go on in the way that has been proved best for them—that is, the way of empire. Can they count on us?

I wish I could answer that question in the full affirmative. I should be very proud of my country if I could. But I cannot. I believe that until all nations come completely out of isolationism we shall live in a miserable war-torn world, more miserable with each succeeding war. Our very misery will drive us to cooperation at last and to the organization of a world society based upon freedom within the world order and the equality of peoples in that order, as the only sane way of living. But we Americans are very far from realizing that today. There are many individuals in America who do realize it. There are others who refuse to realize it and many who cannot realize it. There are more who do not want to be troubled to think about it, and who care nothing for what happens beyond themselves. My reluctant guess, if I must guess, would be that unless this war lasts a very long time, many years more than it looks as though it would, we Americans will not be ready at the end of it to relinquish isolationism except in a limited and modified way, unless there is a new awakening among us.

Nor do I see any great hope of England's being able to change its spots any more quickly, whatever we do about isolationism. The London *Economist* of December 19, 1942, says of us, "The depths and proportions of American ignorance in the most obvious matters of Empire policy and government are unbelievable but it is no use dismissing them on the ground that they are stupid."

It would be folly not to reckon with the fact, therefore, that isolationism is far from dead in America and that in England the notions of some Americans about the right of peoples to be free are still called "stupid."

What would I do if I were an Indian?

Well, first and above all, after reckoning with American isolationism and English imperialism, as they still exist today, I would go to work to expose the great myth of the white man's burden—the myth that more than anything else accounts for isolationism and imperialism.

WHAT AMERICA MEANS TO ME

Americans cling to isolationism really because they don't want to be bothered with the problems of other peoples. When English propaganda cleverly emphasized the immense burden that India is to the Empire, the quarrels among Indian leaders, the impossibility of understanding Indian differences, the patience required and the expense necessary for administration just to keep the Indians from killing each other, American isolationism took on new life. "What!" many Americans began muttering, looking at each other, "are we to get mixed up in all that, too?" When imported Indians began to tour the United States arguing against national independence and fighting each other on the public platforms of this country, as they have done to their own disgrace, it was the cleverest sort of propaganda for Empire. Americans, many of them too ignorant even to suspect propaganda, seeing this exhibition of dissension, shrank back. We have the tradition of keeping out of other people's quarrels. Twice within a generation we have been most unwillingly drawn into European quarrels. It is our terror today lest we add to ourselves the burden of Asia's wars. We want to win against Japan for our own sakes and then get out of Asia as fast as we can. When Englishmen tell us that if we want India free, we must help England bear the burden of Asia, isolationists among us come to new life. We see in India, thanks to England's emphasis on all the possible differences there, something even more troublesome than Europe. We Americans really have no wish to take our share of the white man's burden.

But England, of course, takes a "nobler" view. She feels that it is the white man's duty to bear this burden even at the enormous cost of an expanded empire. We are all familiar with the old argument that were England to leave India tomorrow the Indians would be immediately at each other's throats. Until that is proved false it will remain effective, so deeply has propaganda worked. What the people of India have to get the white man to realize, is that there is not, and there never was, a white man's burden except in the sense that the white man made a burden for himself by trying to force his rule upon reluctant peoples. Any oppressive rule is a burden to the man who tries to enforce it as well as to the man who endures it. Nor is the myth of the white man's burden made less a myth by sentimental talk about its not being a burden because the colored man is the white man's little brother. The man of India and of China and of Africa is not the little brother of the white man, and the self-righteousness which so miscalls him cannot be excused, in these times when men no longer can be excused on the grounds of naïvete or ignorance.

No, the old idea of the white man's burden is a myth, it always was a myth, and it is nothing but a prop to bolster up empire by self-righteousness, and it never was anything else. It is today only a joke. Let us keep it so and laugh it off the earth. And yet unfortunately it is not a joke in its effects, for it is an attitude which more than anything else is maintaining isolationism and imperialism, those two arch enemies of a peaceful and just world society. So long as the people of the United States are convinced that India, Burma, Africa, and all Asiatic and colored peoples are a special problem for the white man, a sufficient number of Americans will retire into isolationism to allow Empire to flourish. We Americans are incurably fond of putting the burdens of life upon others. "Let George do it" is one of the most relished of American sayings, and since Englishmen are so willing to be George and go on with the empire, ostensibly for the benefit of mankind, we will let them go on.

What can you of Asia do with us? I know your despair with the white man, the despair of the peoples of "India and Burma, of Africa and all Asiatic and colored peoples." It is *we* who are *your* burden, that I well know. You must make us realize that you are not our little brothers. You must somehow prove to us beyond any doubt, and prove it practically since that is the only way we can understand it, that you are our equals and in many ways our superiors. We cannot understand moral excellence alone, I will tell you frankly. We do not, therefore, value your moral superiorities as we should. Gandhi we cannot understand, though he is one of the few real saints and great men of our times. We are not able to understand Chiang Kai-shek in some of his great utterances. I admire with all my heart that bold moral affirmation of his made last November. You will remember that he repudiated the notion that China has any wish to become a leader in Asia. He said, "China has no desire to replace western imperialism in Asia with an imperialism of its own or of anyone else." He then went on to call for the effective organization of world unity and for cooperation in the "new inter-dependent world of free nations." There is no nation today fit to lead the world. If my own nation were to set itself up to be the leader, I would be terrified for the other nations. I know my own people, and I love them, and believe in them as a nation, but I know that we, too, are not fit to rule or even to guide the world.

I cannot agree with the president of the United States

TO WIN THE PEACE

Chamber of Commerce when he said, "America will have to take world leadership. No other nation will be physically or mentally capable of doing it. As the most powerful nation on earth, America will have no alternative, in the name of decency or self-interest. . . ."

No, we are not mentally capable of doing it, and if we are only physically capable, we are dangerous. I am not belittling our achievements, which are unique; but they are mainly in the field of science and technology, and they will not suffice to bring peace and prosperity to the world. They have not sufficed in our own country—nor in Europe. The West alone cannot win this war or make a lasting peace. You, the peoples of "India and Burma, of Africa and all the Asiatic and colored countries," must help us, or it will never be done. You must find a way to stop being our little brothers. For until you utterly destroy the notion that you are the white man's burden we cannot have a basis for world peace.

There will be no peace unless it is built upon the primary perception of the equality of mankind. You, in India, must at all costs—yes, at all costs—undertake to make the white man understand this. Moslems and Hindus, and all others, you must undertake this, for the sake of the world, because this quarrel between you has become a world quarrel. It is affecting the freedom of all peoples. You must find ways of coming together, the damage which has been done must be undone, by proving that India can be a union where differences are accepted and allowed for without quarrel and destruction.

Of all the events of this eventful year this matter of India and the loss of the opportunity, through India, of establishing freedom as a principle for relations between peoples, will prove to be the most important for the future. It will nullify, to what extent we cannot now tell, the effect of the magnificent military victories we are winning. It nullifies to some extent—how much who knows?—the effect of China's splendid record. The myth of the white man's burden continues. India will not get her freedom until the myth is destroyed.

How can it be destroyed in India? You must destroy it in your own way, but let me put forth at least a general suggestion. You must find a way of proving that the people of India can function as a free people, in a world of free peoples. Do not say it cannot be done, unless you are willing to remain slaves. You must find the way.

For the future which is the world's only hope today must be based on cooperation between free peoples. This cooperation must be in the form of mutual contribution. It cannot be directive energy from some and obedient energy from others. Whatever the contribution it must come out of the being of the peoples themselves, that is, out of the achievements which they have already made in human development.

Have all peoples achieved something? Yes, all peoples have achieved something. The term "backward peoples" is meaningless. Who is to decide what constitutes a backward people? By the standards of the Chinese, who make human relationships the testing point of civilization, we of the West are backward peoples because we have incessant race and national frictions among our peoples. By the standards of western technologists the Chinese are a backward people because they have not utilized science in shortcuts to labor-saving and conveniences and industrial production. Which of us is right? The Chinese points to the endless wars of the West, to unemployment and insecurity. The American points to lack of roads and factories and plumbing.

The truth is one of those simplicities which confound the learned. We are all backward in some respects, but none is backward in all. The effects of isolation are the same in any country. No country lived in greater isolation than old China, and she developed her own civilization, thinking that no other country was doing the same thing. But old China was not more isolated than America has been, or more isolated than England has been in her imperial self-isolation, or than Germany has been in her race pride, or than Russia has been in her revolution, or than India has been in her retreat into religion. These all developed, each in its own way, a partial civilization. What we are now suffering from is the disjointedness of partial civilizations, each of which seems to its own people the whole, the natural, the perfect, and yet none of which is whole or natural or perfect.

I am not arguing for the amalgamation or the synthesis of civilization. The melting-pot idea is futile in India or the United States. The brew in a melting pot is always boiling over. It will not do for peace or for cooperation. Our own country, the United States, suffices for illustration. We have achieved a union at least within ourselves. Each state, each party, each group, takes pride in its own being, in its difference, as well as in its union with the whole. If we could apply this attitude toward the world at this moment we ourselves might be more ready for a position of leadership among peoples. But we have not been, as a nation, able so to enlarge our vision or so to think of the world as a whole.

There was a time when this war was forcing us so to

think. When we began to send our soldiers all over the world, we began to think rather suddenly of the whole world, not only in the war but for the peace. But isolationism is stronger today than it was a bare three months ago. The danger which I now foresee is that there will be no peoples' determination for world cooperation—propaganda having been very successful for things as they were and are. The average citizen in this country is thinking less of world cooperation today than he was yesterday.

What he fails to realize is that we shall have world organization whether we want it or not, and whether we know it or not. If the average citizens of all countries do not know this fact, they are in peril, for if they cannot cooperate they will be at the mercy of a world organization in which they have no part.

The question is, not whether we shall have world organization, for indeed we are going to have world organization, but only what sort of world organization shall it be? I say positively that we are going to have world organization, on evidence which is open to anyone to discover if he will.

There are men of many nations who are thinking of world organization in terms of world military power. There will be huge military residues left after this war, residues of men and arms and machines to make arms; but more dangerous than that, there will be residues of belief in military force. These will resist disarmament, and to escape disarmament may combine into something which may be called an international army or an international police force. I do not argue the implausibilities of disarmament or the necessity for a world police force to implement peace. I simply say that in the huge military residues left over from this war there will be a terrible weapon in the hands of a group of men, if it is not in the hands of the peoples. In the hands of a group of men it could be used to keep peoples subject for generations more. World organization must not be commandeered by military forces.

Still other groups are thinking in terms of financial power. We have long known that the only true internationalists that the world has had so far have been scientists, artists, and business men. Scientists are supernational because they live in their own world of science, which is the same for all men, whatever their race or nation. Artists live in their world of art, and art knows no distinctions. Neither scientist nor artist is a menace in himself; he is a menace only when his gifts are under malevolent direction. But business men have real power in and by themselves, for what they control is what people must have—food and clothing and produce for all the necessities of life. For these necessities people give money, and so business can control money. There is no other group in the world that has so much potential power as business men have, because they can control both the necessities of life and the money to buy them.

In the past, isolationism curbed this great power of business. When national boundaries were set to protect national business they limited business, too, although this was not their purpose. When the effect of isolationism breaks down in business, some other means must be devised to curb the power of international business. Otherwise, we may have the spectacle of the world's peoples at the mercy of a great international business organization, the peoples' food, their clothing, the very shelter over their heads, dependent upon an inhuman monster of internationalism.

The third possibility of international disaster is that through political domination an international fascist government may follow this war and seize the peace in the name of world order.

Who would be the members of such an organization? They can be found in any country. They would be all those men who have declared themselves, whether openly or not, for rule of empire over what they are pleased to term the "backward" peoples. In Germany and Japan they would be those who would continue to want to rule over the conquered peoples. In Norway there would be Quisling and his followers. In China there would be Wang Ching-wei and his followers. In every country of the earth there can be found at this very moment men who would be brothers to these men, and who would willingly join with them after the war in the name of peace, to make a world government in which the peoples of the earth would be the oppressed.

What then? In alarm at such disaster shall we who are the peoples draw back? There can be no drawing back. The times have forced themselves upon us while we slept. We have waked only sometimes and then only as children wake, to play with our new toys, our airplanes and our fast trains, our telephones and radios. We have shouted to each other across the oceans as children shout over the fence, in glee because of our toys. They are not toys—they are weapons. They will be weapons against us if we draw back in alarm to close our doors again, if we retreat, saying that the situations in the world today are too complex, too difficult, for us to understand.

No, the only hope for the peoples of the world is to

wake, to realize, to understand their danger. World organization is inevitable. If we do not shape it as an organization of peoples and make it an organ of democracy it will be shaped as an organization of our conquerors, and it will be an organ of fascism on a scale which we have not yet seen. And who can say how we could ever be free of it, especially if the three groups combine, the military, the economic and the political? Such combination would only be rational.

What can the peoples do? First of all it is necessary that every means possible be used to awaken people everywhere in large numbers. This must be done by individuals in their own countries and by groups, unresting, unceasing, in their warnings and in their presentation of accumulating facts. It is the special responsibility of the peoples of India and Burma, of Africa and all the Asiatic and colored peoples to force the peoples of the United States and England to wake, by proving to us that isolationism and imperialism are not only impossible, but unnecessary, because the white men have no burden, no little dark brothers.

We people of the United States, we must wake, we must watch, we must not be afraid of what we see. We must watch our own centers of power, concentrating for purposes of war. Millions of men are concentrating under a single military head. Billions of dollars of our tremendous war production funds have gone to a few great corporations. These corporations are expanding enormously. Will this expansion remain idle after the war? Will the medium and small businesses be closed out?

And yet if it is our business and military concentration that threatens the peace, England's political and military concentration will be as dangerous, that concentration which puts into the hands of one government the power over more human beings than any other government in the world.

Today the peoples are pushed into the background by every military victory. A victory or two and we begin to hear such talk in England as "what we have we hold," and here in our own country the head of our National Association of Manufacturers says, "I am not fighting for a quart of milk for every Hottentot," and the new Republican chairman says, "My job is to build an army of voters and I don't believe there are many voters in China or Mongolia that I could get."

There can be no doubt that the United States will win the military war against the Axis. But the peoples of the United Nations must be watchful of the victory.

Yet I would not be true to facts if I allowed it to be thought that I see no awakening, or that there are none to hear the peoples of Asia if they speak to us. There are those among the American and the English people, too, who can hear. I should like to send this reassurance to the people of India on this their Day of Faith, and I should like to send it, too, to the people of China and of Africa and South America and Europe, to all peoples everywhere. There are those in America and England too, who are beginning to wake, and not all of us are afraid of that awakening.

We in America come of liberty-loving ancestry. Our fore-fathers fought for liberty, and we can fight again. All over our land the awakening to freedom is coming like the first ripples of wind over the ocean. It is coming among colored people in the United States, it is coming among women's groups, it is coming among teachers and school children and labor unions, in little towns and villages. Nor is it only here. There are such groups as that small but growing peoples party in Canada, the Cooperative Commonwealth Federation, which has taken a clear stand on the immediate freedom of the people of India as a necessary part of the freedom of all peoples.

Yes, the tide is rising, but it must rise more quickly, quickly enough so that the victory to come, perhaps sooner than we think, may be a true victory for us all. Each of us in his place can add strength and swiftness to the rising tide of the peoples.

The peoples of the earth must wake. Let us know each other and recognize each other's voices, and uphold each other, in all lands, among all races, in order that *we* may win the peace.

14. CAN THE ENGLISH TRUST US?

THE debacle of Pearl Harbor, Hong Kong and Singapore, of Malaya and Burma, showed us that neither Americans nor Englishmen know enough about the peoples of Asia, either foes or allies, for war or peace. Such age-long ignorance cannot be quickly mended. Language alone is barrier enough between peoples—and of our allies, Russia and China have two of the most difficult languages in the world. In the immense need for somehow learning in a day, in a month, in a year, what we must know, and ought to have known long ago, it has been a great relief to think that at least one great ally, England, speaks our tongue. In our emergency need for more knowledge of many countries and peoples, it has been a comfort to think, "At least, we English and Americans can understand each other."

But this comfort has been shaken by the realization of a peculiar situation growing up between the Americans and the English. In spite of insistent demands that no signs of disunity between the English and ourselves shall be recognized, it has become apparent that among the grass roots of the people in the United States there

An article in *The New York Times Magazine*, April 18, 1943.

CAN THE ENGLISH TRUST US?

is far too much distrust and doubt of England. There is similar distrust and doubt growing up in England toward us.

So extreme has this distrust become among Americans that all sorts of undesirables are using so-called "anti-English feeling" to promote their own schemes of isolationism, and the "new American imperialism." This is resulting in a state of mind in many English so sensitive that they have come to the point, consciously or unconsciously, of an exclusive jealousy, of demanding a total exclusion of all other interests as the sign of complete loyalty to England. Thus they make it a sign of anti-British feeling when anyone pleads the cause of China as an ally also, and talk of the possibilities of negotiating with India as a wise war measure is taken by sensitive British souls as merely rank enmity toward England. Now the absurdity has spread in turn to the Chinese who feel that American loyalty to the English must be taken as a sign of being anti-Chinese.

And furthermore what may have very disastrous effects on America's future, is the eagerness of English statesmen to insist on Hitler as the chief enemy, which has resulted in a demand upon us to put Japan as only our second enemy. The great climax of the war, Churchill has said, is to be the moment when Hitler is beaten. And yet all thinking Americans know that, necessary as the vanquishment of Hitler is to us, it is hardly probable that the great climax of the war will come for us until Japan is vanquished.

But such is the state of affairs now between ourselves and England that only the reckless dare to mention these things. It is time for sensible American citizens to take stock of the situation by asking some frank questions.

WHAT AMERICA MEANS TO ME

Do we understand the English and do they understand us? In spite of our common tongue, do we speak the same language?

Before one can proceed to any frank discussion these days one has first to dismiss the hush-hushers, all those who dread and fear any frankness and would ignore at any cost all troublesome truths. The universality and persistence of this breed is shown by the famous three monkeys of the ancient East, who sit to this day with hands pressed over their eyes, ears and mouths. To see nothing, to hear nothing, to say nothing is to know nothing these monkeys tell us, and to know nothing is to believe that nothing is there. For example, the Americans who declare that it is helping the Axis to mention lynchings in our own South belong to this school of monkeys. They refuse to hear, to see, to mention the fact of lynchings, while they will not lift a finger to prevent lynchings. They also ignore the fact that all over the world our Axis enemies snatch at news of our lynchings and make it public, even if our own newspapers do not.

But why specify a country, my own or any other? The three monkeys can be found anywhere. Let us therefore in the spirit of a common sense of which monkeys are incapable, examine our present situation as regards England.

When I say England, I mean the English people, and when I say the English people I mean all English people. The people of England within a much more limited space than ours are as diverse in their opinions as we are. They can afford to be even more diverse than we are in mind, for they do not have to struggle against our diversities of race, tradition, religion, food and customs.

CAN THE ENGLISH TRUST US?

They, therefore, speak with much more freedom than we can, argue with each other far more publicly, disagree with a plainness, whether between husband and wife or between liberal and conservative, that could never be done here without name-calling, and all this without fear of anybody hush-hushing them on the ground of giving the Axis comfort. Nobody believes the English are disunited, however ferociously they disagree with each other, for everybody knows they are agreed on one thing, and it is that England is to be preserved at all costs, even when those costs are the sacrifice of everything that is personal, including personal opinions. Even Hitler must now know that for the sake of England the rich and the upper classes will give up wealth and position, and that for the sake of England, labor will give up labor's rights and follow even leaders whom they denounce.

With such unity as this we cannot compete. It is not yet true that for the sake of America the Negro-haters will give up race prejudice, and it is not likely that for the sake of America the isolationist will give up his isolationism, nor for that matter can it be proved that for the sake of America either the Republicans or the Democrats will give up their politics.

Here, in a nutshell, is the difference between the English and us. The English are a united people, indivisible in their great single love of England. And England is much—it is far more than the soil, though the soil is part of it, as the soil is part of China. There is a family quality in England's people that there is also in China's people. The English can trust each other, even while they bitterly disagree. The most intelligent, the most outspoken criticism of the British Government's policy in India has been made by English newspapers. Englishmen have taken a stand on the freedom of India which is far more advanced, more sensible, more understanding, than we in America have taken. Let those who have not followed the English press—and I wish every American did—read in the February 26 issue of *The Manchester Guardian Weekly,* the editorial entitled "Mr. Gandhi," and the editorial entitled "Commonsense or Prestige?" in the February 27 issue of *The New Statesman and Nation.* Here in varying kinds of minds one sees a common realism that is very far removed indeed from the hush-hushing of the three monkeys or from our own, for that matter, on this particular subject of India and the war.

The English men and English women who profoundly disagree with the Churchill policy toward India can yet, after they have voiced their disagreement, allow Churchill to go on, sure that in the long run and not too long run at that perhaps others, if not Churchill, will carry out a policy toward India which will be to the best interests of a contended Empire. Our own southern forces cannot so trust Roosevelt or those who follow him on the matter of our own subject people, the Negroes. A contented United States is not their aim—their aim is to preserve intact the distance between the white man and the colored in the United States primarily and in the world secondarily. England's white supremacy is maintained not for itself but merely as a technique of Empire, and when it is not needed as a technique of Empire, it does not exist. It is no more beautiful or right for that, but at least it is not so deeply founded nor actually so dangerous as the conviction in many white

CAN THE ENGLISH TRUST US?

southern minds here that a colored skin is an actual sign of inferiority, whenever it is found.

The English habit of outspokenness is one of their finest qualities, even though it is sometimes disconcerting abroad. There has been in England very frank criticism of the American policy in North Africa, for example, and more frank criticism, accompanied by considerable disgust, at the behavior of our white troops in England toward our colored troops there. English plain people have simply refused to observe the color bar in England, and they have become silent, though remaining rebellious, only because of the sternest orders from those above that for the sake of America's tender feelings as allies, there is to be no more spoken criticism. But anything more eloquent than the average Englishman's silence when he is forbidden to speak cannot be imagined. It has to be seen. It leaves no doubt that he disagrees with us, and that he will continue to disagree with us while in silence. The air with which my English friends refuse to discuss the "colored question here in your country," is so noisy with disapproval that I frequently beg them to speak in order to make it possible for me to go on breathing the air in the same room with them.

Yes, the unity of the English is an amazing unity, while in America there are all sorts of persons who do not love America more than they love their prejudices and their parties. One result of this difference between the English and ourselves is that the English can move with a directness impossible to us, because they need not be on guard among themselves. The English are now moving toward the future with a sureness and a swiftness far beyond us. Will our far slower pace, even though it is in the same direction as England's, open a division between the English people and ourselves? Can so simple a thing as mere speed at arriving at decisions, at implementing these decisions, have so dire a result as this? That there is this difference in speed is undeniable. England has already achieved a unity with Russia, for example, that is as yet impossible to us because of our preoccupation with communism and our own communists. The English people are so sure of the Englishness even of their own communists that they cannot regard them as a menace. We are not so sure of ours.

Our speed toward the goal of victory is delayed by such impediments. The isolationists, for example, are now beginning to make hay again since Churchill's last speech gave them sunshine. Churchill's suggestion that there be a Council of Asia and a Council of Europe left the way open for a Council of the Americas, and isolationism, regionalism, tribalism, inevitable sources of future wars, lifted their hydra heads at once. Yet what that speech really said ought to have given every American pause for thought. What it said was plain enough—that England is no longer going to wait for America to make up her mind. England is going ahead with her own shape of the world to come, and that shape is to be built primarily around a strong relationship between herself and Russia. Russia has shown the realistic English people a realistic Russian people—a people who can fight for their own as the English have fought for their own. It is a simple war, this war to keep what one has, but that is the war the English are fighting and it is the war the Russians are fighting. The English and the Russians can, therefore, understand each other. They can each live with the sort of governments they have, because they

CAN THE ENGLISH TRUST US?

know that scratch either Churchill or Stalin and under whatever surface there is you will find beneath it simply England and Russia. English people and Russian people know this and in their knowledge they are united. England knows that Russians are fighting for Russia as the English people are fighting for England.

Neither people has this same bond with us. They trust us in the war, of course, but can they trust us in the peace? For they do not know what is under our surface. Scratch any of us, from Roosevelt down to a little man on the street and you never quite know what you will find—a democrat or a republican, an isolationist, a communist, an imperialist or a new dealer. The Englishman is disturbed by this. He can take a great deal of variety of surface, but he likes to be sure the inside is solid. That solidity he is now finding in Russia instead of in America.

Now to any patriotic American this is a profoundly distressing thing. We have always taken for granted our kinship with the English. We have disliked and do dislike some things that are English—perhaps that very surety which they possess as the result of their long unity of blood and tradition is something we secretly envy even while we sometimes dislike its effects.

And yet, in spite of this and of our awareness at the same time of their dislike of much that is ours, we have always felt and have needed to feel that we are allied to the English. Even the strong strains of Irish blood in us, and of other professional England-haters, never really shake the conviction that the English and the Americans belong on the same side of the fence.

It is unthinkable to us at any time that the English and ourselves could be on opposite sides of the fence in a war. But is there danger now that we may be on different sides of the fence in the peace? I think there is, and the possibility is so monstrous, so dangerous, that we ought to examine into it and see why it can exist even in the imagination. For if England has needed us and if we have needed England in the war, we shall doubly need each other in the peace. The English began by stressing very much the alliance between themselves and us. There has been constant pressure from Englishmen in high places to shape an Anglo-American world. We have resisted that pressure fairly steadily as a people, in spite of Presidential acquiescence, believing rather in a United Nations world, and that an Anglo-American alliance alone would simply mean a larger unit for the attack in the next war—it would not avert another war. It has been to our credit that we, more than the English, have thought in world terms at least in this one matter. It would be more to our credit had we moved forward to definite plans and implementation as a result of our belief.

The result of our delay, however, in putting forward any clear plans and in devising any workable implementation of them has been that England has gone ahead of us. She has enlarged her world to include Russia. It has been a necessity for her to do so, failing the strong union she desired to make with us. She has taken the lead in the alliance and the reason for this has been her growing distrust of us for the future—a distrust based not only on our apparent determination to stay out of an exclusive alliance with her, but our apparent wish to stay out of any alliance—that is, our old predilection for isolationism.

If England needed more proof of our position she got

CAN THE ENGLISH TRUST US?

it a short time ago when two Republicans and two Democrats introduced a resolution which would put the Senate on record as "advising" that the United States take the initiative in calling together representatives of our allies "for the purpose of forming an organization of the United Nations." Even so mild and tentative a gesture as this has been opposed openly and loudly with a stupidity which causes an agony of embarrassment to all sensible Americans.

The three monkeys may not know it, but isolationism in this country is growing by leaps and bounds and there is no concealing it. The future of the world is being shaped in recognition of it. Wise Englishmen, thinking of the peace that now seems not too far off, a peace frightening with its problems, have arrived, with a speed imperceptible to us, at the conclusion that they had better build plans which take into account our isolationism. They are determined not again to waste a lot of time at the peace table with us, only to have the work undone when our representatives come home.

I wish, as an American, that I could say that they were wrong. I fear that the English are only sensible in making what alliances they can, and in leaving us out to the extent that our failure to cooperate will not cripple future world cooperation. I think that English people feel that a world based on full cooperation would be the best of all because they think it would be the best for England, as a matter of simple common sense. But if full cooperation is impossible, then they must still think first of England.

Would that we were so realistic! But instead of thinking about the sort of world which would be best for America, we are thinking of isolationism and race prejudice and business greed and the American way of living and keeping our boys at home and a dozen other ideas, all of which we love better than the idea of America itself, a country of free people that can be secure only in a world of free peoples cooperating with each other in mutual responsibility and to mutual advantage.

And our refusal to come out of isolationism has made even England a lesser power for a better world than she might be. How, for example, can England contemplate the price of a free India and the end of the colonial system unless we are willing for the sake of the principle of the freedom of all peoples, to take our part in the reconstruction which such freedom would mean? We have offered no help to those English men and women, and they are many, who believe in that principle and would be willing and eager to see India free and all peoples free, and to work for that freedom, but who cannot work alone.

Once again our longing for retreat into irresponsibility is about to hold back the progress of mankind. We still do not come out with the clear statement of what sort of world America wants and will pledge herself to bring into being.

How can England trust us?

15. TWO AMERICANS

I. THOMAS JEFFERSON

THE great war began in ages past—at a moment symbolized, perhaps, by the old story of Cain and Abel, when Cain turned on God and asked with such scorn and anger, "Am I my brother's keeper?" You know what Cain was like—an arrogant, aggressive go-getter sort of a fellow, a man who liked a quarrel, a hunter, a man who enjoyed stalking his prey. And Abel was a farmer and a worker, a quiet man who believed in peace, but didn't intend to be run over by Cain, either.

All through the ages of man's history Cain and Abel have been at war—Cain trying to rule and Abel resisting his rule and trying to maintain his right to live quietly and at peace, without being subject to Cain. Whether Cain and Abel were two individual men who once lived doesn't matter. They have lived millions of times in millions of men, in every country and every race—the men who want to rule and the men who want to be free. Sometimes Cain is a certain nation, sometimes a certain race, sometimes a certain class, sometimes even a certain man. But Cain has always lived, and Abel has always

The first section of this chapter is part of a speech delivered at a meeting in honor of Mary McLeod Bethune in Washington, March 8, 1943. The second section is a speech delivered at Town Hall, New York, March 17, 1943.

WHAT AMERICA MEANS TO ME

lived; they live today and the relation between them is the same, Cain asking still whether or not he is his brother's keeper, and is he to care what happens to men like Abel, and Abel standing steadily firm that he, too, is a man and deserves a man's freedom.

It would be easier surely if we could point to a single nation or a single race for the eternal Cain, but we cannot. In China, I remember, white men excluded Chinese upon Chinese soil from certain parks and buildings and organizations, and it made the Chinese very angry—rightfully so. But in Malaya, where the Chinese were the successful business men, they excluded the people of Malaya in exactly the same way which they felt was so wicked in China. They had buildings and clubs and organizations which they forbade to the Malayans. I remember the Tiger Swimming Pool in Malaya, which had the sign on it, "Chinese Only." It was a local thing, but it stood for something terrifyingly large. It stood for a whole group of people who were able, in this case because of their wealth as well as their nationality, to exclude another group even upon the second group's soil.

But no nation has a clean record. England has India and Africa, we have our own American Negroes, France has her wretched colonials, Germany has the Jews, Japan the Koreans, Russia the people who could not agree with Communism—everywhere in skin of every hue, there is still being repeated the old story of Cain and Abel, over and over again. The great war of humankind is the war between those two, the oppressed and the oppressor, fought and never yet won.

Even here in America we cannot say that this war for the liberation of man is between one race and another. The longer I live here, the more I inquire into our own life, the more I see that here, too, Cain is not always a white man, nor Abel a colored one. It would be much simpler if it could divide us as clearly as that. It would be much easier to fight for the colored person as always the one oppressed and the white man as always the oppressor. In some parts of our country this is so, and the fight can be made as simply as that. But these are local spots, and even here the fight is not always clear. I have myself been sometimes confused by discovering, even in the places where discrimination is the worst, that part of the discrimination is carried on by colored people, too—colored people a little lighter than some others, colored people connected with certain white people in one way or another. The issue is not clear. I believe with all my heart that jimcrow is wicked and I know that it is a rotten core in our society. I know that we cannot say that we are a full democracy so long as jimcrow exists anywhere in our country. I will fight against it and refuse to countenance it in all ways that I can, as long as I live. And yet I know that were all jimcrow laws to be abolished tomorrow, the war for the liberation of mankind would still not be won here. There would still be those not free, not equal.

The war for the liberation of man is the sum of all the struggles everywhere of men and women trying to be free, not only of race discrimination, but of economic discrimination and sex discrimination and religious discrimination and political discrimination. Time and again this great war for the freedom of mankind has broken out into military battles, as it is doing today. There will be these military outbursts so long as we will not recognize, will not acknowledge, that mankind must be free.

WHAT AMERICA MEANS TO ME

And by freedom I mean men and women of every race and color, living unafraid in a commonwealth, a nation, a world where the common good of peoples is of the first importance, and not the maintenance of a class or a race or a nation at the expense of others.

We are today having to fight in many countries a military war. Our young men are living and dying on foreign soil. Our material wealth is being poured out for people we have never seen, people in Europe, people in Asia and Africa. You and I earn money not to use for ourselves, but beyond our necessities to use for other peoples not of our blood and kind. To make this worth doing, we must be sure of our own being, and that what we believe is that in which all peoples believe, the freedom of peoples.

There are those who do not believe in this freedom, persons in every country, and such persons have seized the power in Germany and Japan and Italy. But everywhere the common man and his family believe in freedom for all people. I have lived in many countries of the world and talked with their peoples often, and never yet have I seen the people, the everyday people, of any country, who did not, when one of them felt himself able to speak, want to be free and want all others to be free in the great commonwealth sense of the word freedom.

In spite of our discriminatory behavior toward some of our people, here in America more than in any other country the concept of the freedom of mankind is still the clearest and the strongest. This I think is because here have lived so many men and women free enough to be able to speak out again and again for the freedom of all, at times when such freedom was threatened.

TWO AMERICANS

Of all those who have spoken none was greater than Thomas Jefferson. Let me talk of him for a little while, if for nothing else than to acknowledge my own debt to him. For having lived most of my life away from my own country, in a civilization very different from this one, it was necessary when I came home to discover my own country and to find where its greatness lies. Thomas Jefferson, more than any other figure, has shown me the greatness of America.

You will remember how they say he looked—that tall, lean, red-haired man from Virginia. American to the core he was, with his dry humor, his patience, his industry, his practical mind, his carefulness about money, his shrewdness and his immense humanity and kindness. He inherited great lands in Virginia, and one of his most notable works was breaking up the system of great land holdings which he felt made it impossible for democracy to exist. Primogeniture—that law whereby only the eldest son could inherit the estate—kept the lands of Virginia in the hands of a few. It meant that there was a permanent aristocracy, which if it went on would make impossible self-government by free men. Jefferson was trained as a lawyer and his first blow against primogeniture was a bill making it possible for all the heirs in a family to inherit land, so that the great estates were divided again and again and made available for sale to those who could buy them—that is, the land passed into the hands of the people. "If the eldest son," Jefferson said, "could eat twice as much, or do double work; it might be a natural evidence of his right to a double portion, but being on a par in his powers and wants, with his brothers and sisters, he should be on a par also in the partition of the patrimony."

WHAT AMERICA MEANS TO ME

Jefferson wrote the Declaration of Independence not exactly as it stands today. His first draft was a great prose poem of anger and accusation against tyranny and of determination for the rights of man:

> When in the course of human events
> it becomes necessary for one people
> to dissolve the political bonds
> which have connected them with another,
> and to assume
> among the powers of the earth,
> the separate and equal station
> to which the laws of nature
> and of nature's God
> entitle them,
> a decent respect to the opinions of mankind requires
> that they should declare the causes
> which impel them to the separation.

With this magnificent opening he goes on, as who among us does not remember, to that great declaration for humanity:

> We hold these truths
> to be self-evident,
> that all men are created equal,
> that they are endowed by their Creator
> with inherent and unalienable rights,
> that among these
> are life, liberty, and the pursuit of Happiness.

Saul Padover, in his fine book *Jefferson,* says, "Ordinarily the triplex of political values included life, liberty and property. By substituting the 'pursuit of happiness' for 'property' Jefferson broke with the traditional concept and laid the foundation for a unique commonwealth of justice and freedom and security."

He laid that foundation for us and through us for every human creature now without freedom in this whole world. The foundation is here, whether the building is complete or not. Such a foundation exists nowhere else in the world.

And then having laid this foundation he went to work to build upon it as best he could in his day and his time. He revised the whole body of our law, clarifying the involved thought and simplifying the absurd legal language.

He was the founder of our public school system, for he believed that the people must be educated or democracy cannot continue to exist, that individual talent, wherever it is found, must be developed, and that all children must be educated at common expense if by no other means. He wrote that great bill for religious freedom which caused such consternation because not only did it give a man the right to worship God as he pleased but gave him the right, too, to worship no God, if he so pleased. He believed that Church and State should be entirely separate, so that these two great powers, political and religious, could never join hands to oppress the people. He saw that to have such permanent separation it must be law that a man could worship God in his own fashion, or not at all, and that the State must be powerless over such freedom.

To introduce such ideas of freedom made Jefferson at once the most hated and the most loved of men. Those who hated freedom hated him. But the common people, that is, most of the people, of any country in the world loved him and knew that in him they had their friend.

What I found deepest and best in his life was his

ability to think in terms of all mankind. It is a quality which we all need today. We are in so violent a battle at this moment that it is our danger that we think this battle is the whole war. No battle is a whole war. Each battle must be fought and none must be put aside, lest the war be lost by so much. But the real war in which we fight is the war for the freedom of mankind, the right of people everywhere to live in security, to develop in safety to the fullest of their capacity, and this capacity, though it varies with the individual, does not vary with race or nationality. All peoples are created equal, if all persons are not, and it is the recognition of this equality of peoples which is necessary for freedom.

Thomas Jefferson did not speak for some of us but for all of us. Colored men and women were honored guests in his home if they were men and women to be honored. He was a true American and the tradition which he established is the tradition of our country, however often it is broken. Our country is founded upon human equality and upon the freedom of peoples.

It is at those springs in our own history that we must refresh ourselves today. They are not always clear or peaceful springs. The war has never yet been won in our own country even while we fight it in and for the world. It is well to remember this, indeed we must remember it, for we know it every day in a thousand ways. You know it who live in Washington, the city which ought to be in every way the stronghold where democracy is practiced as well as preached, and yet where it is not practiced, so long as discrimination persists. The war is not won, but here is the strength to give us all resolution—if it is not won, neither is it lost. There are countries in which today it is lost until a new generation grows up, lost unless the rebirth can come out of this country and the few other countries where the fight for the freedom of the peoples can still be made.

Shall any battle be delayed here at home because there are battles abroad? No, it is essential for victory everywhere that here in our own country we all press on to destroy everything that denies equality. Victory can come only if all fronts are fought at the same time.

Thomas Jefferson more than any other one man, perhaps, fixed our nation upon the foundations of a workable democracy. He did well in his time, let us do well in ours. Upon that foundation let us build a structure of true democracy, fighting against everything that would make it false, fighting with a sense of the whole, as he did. It is inequality which we must destroy, not a certain group of human beings. When a nation has descended to murder in order to instill a new idea, all of that nation has always been weakened thereby. Russia was weakened when she did so, China was weakened when she did so, the British Empire was weakened when it did so. Our hands are little stained as yet, because we have fought a more positive war for democracy, for equality, for the right of individuals to live and to be free. The stains we have are the stains of single individual lynchings, not the mass murders of hundreds and thousands. If we believe in the worth of the human individual, which is the real meaning of human equality and of democracy itself, then we must achieve our practice of our beliefs not by the physical destruction even of our enemies, but by other means. And there, too, we do well to read of Jefferson, for he had his enemies, but he did not murder them, and he died well beloved of the nation.

WHAT AMERICA MEANS TO ME

What is it to be American today? I think it is to maintain steadfastly our belief in the peoples of the earth, in their right to be free in a commonwealth of the world, in their right to develop themselves, with the help of all but without the rule of any, guarded in their weaknesses and cooperative in their strengths. We are fighting for a world in which every people can live in cooperation with every other. It can be done, for peoples are simple enough at heart. They love freedom above all else, and with freedom assured will work, as neighbors do, in a community where all are assured of each other's good will safe, to maintain their mutual safety.

II. Abraham Lincoln

I had to discover Abraham Lincoln for myself. My ancestors lived near the western edge of pre-Civil War Virginia, and when the war came and the State separated into two, the line was drawn straight through the middle of our region. I was, and I have always been glad of it, born over the border in West Virginia, in that part of the country which, theoretically, at least, sided with the Union. I say theoretically, because as a matter of fact, although partly in West Virginia, the feeling of the whole family was with Virginia. The consequence of this was that I grew up not allowed to read Harriet Beecher Stowe, and whenever the Civil War was talked of, my parents, who were children during that war, remarked with bitterness that the South would have freed the slaves anyway gradually and were indeed already doing so. If someone brought up the name of Abraham Lincoln my father's unfailing comment was, "Lincoln was a very much over-rated man." What I have come to

TWO AMERICANS

know and to feel about Abraham Lincoln, therefore, is entirely my own responsibility.

I say that, and yet I know that while in my parents' American home in China there was no recognition of Lincoln's greatness, yet elsewhere I heard rumors of it. Certainly the Chinese among whom I lived knew very little about America or the Civil War, and yet somehow even to those remote regions there had come rumors of Abraham Lincoln. I think the first time I heard one of those rumors was when I was quite a young child, perhaps not more than nine or so, and I heard it from an old Chinese gentleman who was my tutor in Chinese. I don't think he knew anything more about America than that, for I never heard him make the slightest comment on anything else American. But one day when we were reading a little story of a runaway slave and I did not understand the two characters for slave, *nu-p'oh,* he stopped and said solemnly, "In your country the dark people were slaves until A-ba-la-hen Lin Kung said, 'There shall be no more slaves now and henceforward forever in America.' Now do you understand the word 'slave?' "

I had, later, a little book of easy Chinese prepared by some Chinese writer, in which were stories of the great men of all countries, and Abraham Lincoln was the only American in that book. There was a picture of him, I remember, a very badly printed, blotchy picture of that tall, plain man, never handsome even at his best, except in the beauty of his nobility.

What was remembered of Abraham Lincoln, what was known of him on the other side of the world which knew little of us in those days, was that he had set people free. That news had gone around the world with the speed of light.

I don't know whether Abraham Lincoln knew exactly what he was doing when he freed the slaves. Perhaps he did it only as a war measure. The war, you remember, dragged along without any heart in it. Nobody seemed to want to fight. There was everything to fight for, seemingly—the Union, the preservation of a country whole—but the idea of union, even of country, did not seem enough to make men want to fight. Patriotism in the North was not actually as strong a motive as the property motive of the South, that South which was ready to secede rather than give up its economy based upon slave labor. There are not many motives in the world, of course, as strong as the property motive.

There were even plenty of people, accustomed to the small compact nations of Europe, who thought that perhaps this great expanse of America should not be one country, that it might be better if it were divided into nations instead of states. But others were determined that the continual bickering and quarreling between the little nations of Europe should not be repeated here and they were determined to keep the country whole and large, and among these was Abraham Lincoln.

Yet how could he fire many men's hearts with this idea? He could not. The war was badly fought, for the Northerners fought on the whole listlessly, even hiring men to fight in their places. There was actual danger that the South might win. The Southerners, supported by the slaves upon their lands, could fight and be supplied with endless reserves. I suppose that Lincoln began to see that men who had at their beck and call thousands of subject creatures whom they could force to work for them and feed them while they fought, were a menace to any country, to any nation. Thus supported, they could devote their time to rule. They could be a caste which if not broken up would go on to greater and greater power. He foresaw, perhaps, that if these men of the South won the war, it would not be only the war which they won. They would win the peace.

He determined to destroy that base upon which such men lived. The greatest blow for freedom that was ever struck in the world's history, perhaps, was when Abraham Lincoln decided that the slaves of the South were to be free and he freed them. The South collapsed. The gentlemen who could spend their time fighting, sure of supplies from slave-tended lands, began to starve and go ragged. Their homes began to fall into ruin and their families to be hungry. Their morale was broken. The war was really won by the pen upon the paper which wrote down these words, "are and henceforward shall be free."

Of course the slaves might have reasoned that they were better fed and better cared for as slaves than as free men. This was undoubtedly true in many instances. It is probably quite true that most slaves *were* better off, physically, slave than free. I don't think they thought about that. I think when that magic word *freedom* rang through the air they did not care whether they ate or drank again. They simply put down their hoes. Even grateful ones who loved their masters and mistresses took their freedom, although more than a few times they continued to work on and to care for those whom they loved. But none of them rejected their freedom. I have not heard of any who said, "I don't want to be free." Doubtless there were some, for there are always ignorant, bewildered people and it would be natural if some of these were afraid of having to look out for themselves. But the vast majority snatched at freedom, even when it meant no food, no shelter, nothing except their bodies for their possession.

I suppose Abraham Lincoln knew that was what would happen. He was very wise in the ways of men. He knew how people think and feel. Doubtless he knew that deeper than anything else in the hearts of men everywhere is the wish for simple freedom—freedom without any promises even of protection, of food, of security—just freedom. He knew that those people, so long bond, would leave even comfortable sheltered places where masters were kind, if they could only be free.

Had Japan been a tenth as wise as Abraham Lincoln, had Hitler been a hundredth part as sensible, we today, the United States and England, would not have a chance in this war. Had those two enemies of ours coveted the lands upon which subject peoples dwell today and had they whispered the magic word *freedom* to those peoples, they might have set half the world against us in a moment. But they have lost because they attacked lands already free, and because they have enslaved peoples accustomed to freedom. By this one thing alone, if by no other, they are doomed. They have misread the hearts and minds of men. By their enslavement of the peoples whom they have made subject by force of arms, they have aroused against themselves a greater force than can be found in any army, in any weapon. It is this—the will of men everywhere to be free.

Let us learn today from Abraham Lincoln, as we fight this war still so far from victory. He could not win that war until he lit the fire in the hearts of men and women enslaved. Nothing had been enough to make men rise up and shout aloud for victory until that moment. A few men like war and enjoy it as a game. But most men and all women hate war. They will not fight with their whole hearts unless they are set aflame. And the torch is always the same words. Whisper those words and men and women will shout them aloud and sing them as they march. The words are simple but they are the most potent in the universe—they are the spiritual dynamite of victory.

The words? "All persons held as slaves . . . are and henceforward shall be free."

16. WHAT AMERICA MEANS TO ME

I SHOULD like here to tell as simply and as clearly as I can what America means to me and how I feel about being an American.

I have not always lived here. Nearly the whole of my life, all except the last few years, in fact, has been lived on the other side of the world. My American parents took me there when I was three months old. My tongue learned another language before it learned English. My eyes were accustomed first not to the faces of my own people but to alien faces, although I did not know them alien and do not know them alien now. But those first impressions of childhood are always very strong. I was taught in another civilization before I came to be part of my own. My unconscious memories are of another country and another people. My own country and my own people I have approached only consciously and with full awareness of their meaning.

Now all this is of no particular importance except that it may be interesting to know how our country seems to an American coming home to it freshly in full

A speech delivered at a U.S. Treasury Bond Rally at Allentown, Pennsylvania, February 24, 1943.

maturity after half a lifetime away, and that half a lifetime spent not in a savage or uncivilized country, but in the oldest and one of the most civilized countries of the world.

The physical face of America is very beautiful. Not all of our country is beautiful, nor of any country, but we have as high a proportion of the beautiful, certainly, as any large country. Traveling westward over the mountains and deserts, traveling south, driving over New England and over the eastern states, my heart has often filled with pride in the natural beauty we possess. But China is a very beautiful country, too, and I was accustomed to natural beauty, though valuing it none the less for that. I soon began to try to discover the particular, American quality of our fine landscape. I found it in its naturalness.

The beauty of older countries, such as China and India and even England, although England is still young compared to those two, is in the humanized aspect of the country. When a people has lived on a piece of earth's surface for thousands of years, that land begins to have a human sort of look, a lived-upon look, like a very old house through which generations of the same family have passed. That is the beauty of the old countries of China and India. Man has become a part of their landscape. His houses fit the contours of hills and rocks. Chinese houses, especially, have assumed architectural lines that seem molded to the shapes of mountains and valleys and plains. You can look at a Chinese landscape and not even see the houses and villages for a while, until your eye can pick them out, so perfectly are they a part of the whole. Chinese farmers, working in their fields, their brown backs bare under the sun, seem part of the land. Their work garments are nearly always of a blue cotton cloth that is the same blue as the sky. Nothing startles, even the homes and gardens of the rich are planned carefully in the same harmony with an old nature.

Here in our country the real beauty is the untamed beauty of a nature not yet in harmony with man. We have not come to grips with our country yet. We have not made even the soil our own as the people have in China, where for forty centuries men have been farmers upon the same farms and yet today the earth into which they sow seed and from which they reap harvest is as rich as ever, enriched literally by human waste from the living and by the flesh and blood and bones of the millions of the dead of many generations. We use our country ruthlessly, and she retaliates sometimes with tired fields and worn out farms. We have not yet learned to fertilize our land deeply.

Our landscape is not in full harmony with us yet, nor we with it. Our houses are what we build, each man after his own idea, and without much regard to the hills and valleys and plains around us. Only in a few places in America, and I am glad that our region is one of them, do the people seem to have learned to build houses that are part of the landscape.

And yet this very individualism has something American about it, as American as our untamed natural mountains and streams. Every man says to himself that he has the right to make the kind of house he wants and he does. What I felt then, before I knew my own people, was that only a very individualistic, outspoken, forthright people could live in the houses I saw upon our landscape. Only a very natural sort of people could they be.

When I came to know better the people who lived in those houses, I was surprised that America is not richer than she is. On the other side of the world I had heard a great deal about our fabulous standard of living. China, and indeed all Asiatic persons, said that they were excluded from our country lest they bring down our standard of living. I don't know what I expected, exactly, but somehow I had the notion from all this hearsay that all Americans, perhaps, lived as only the rich do in China.

The first blow to this idea came, perhaps, when I saw Americans doing crude labor on docks and railways and in the places where such labor has to be done—a thing which no white man in the East would have considered possible for him. Then I began to see the true American idea that labor has nothing to do with standards of living. The man who works all day digging and hauling may go home at night to a comfortable house, which may have a refrigerator and a furnace and a bathroom and all such conveniences. Well, that seemed splendid to me until I went on to discover that after all most houses in America don't have furnaces and refrigerators and bathrooms. These things are still luxuries, even here. Of course I knew very well that they are not necessities for comfort or cleanliness, for very rich people indeed in China may live with none of these things, and yet live in great magnificence. So, even with all our conveniences we are not too rich in comparison with other peoples. One needs only to travel in parts of the South or the Dakotas, for example, and in many other parts of our country to realize that our standards of living are not yet high enough and not universal enough. They are not much higher than those of peacetime China, to tell the truth, if we measure comfort in terms of adequate shelter, security, and good food.

Now this discovery that our country is not sitting in the midst of all the other countries like a millionaire in a slum, as I thought she was, was of great comfort to me. I was glad and I am glad to find that our problems are, by and large, still the problems of all peoples—how to get enough jobs for everybody, how to get our children educated, how to provide for our old, how to get our taxes paid. In short, I began to feel very much at home in my own country as soon as I discovered that ours is not a fabulous land, not a place of incredible wealth, but a country full of active struggling human beings, trying to make ends meet and get some pleasure out of life and do the best we can for our family and neighbors and friends. That is the way it is everywhere else, I can assure you. In some ways we do get along better than other people do, mainly in the things that science has done for us. In other ways we have succeeded less well than some people—Japan, for example, has a higher rate of literacy than we have, even with our splendid school system, and individual security is higher in China than it is here, because of the strong family group.

Well, taking it all in all, I liked my country better for being a nation where the people still were struggling for more security and better health and better homes and better government. Today the fact that we are a nation of plain people not in a position of great advantage over others, not in fact as rich as some other countries in natural resources, or in individual accumulation, makes us all the stronger as a democracy. We are not hampered by empire, for example. We do not have to hold other peoples down by force, or control unwilling territories by arms and bombers. We can say and prove it by what we are that we believe in democracy and are ready to fight for it when it is threatened.

As I became familiar with our landscape and our ways, I began to find out what our people are like and I could contrast them with other peoples I knew. What are we like, we Americans? I take it for granted that we know that we are not better or worse than other folk, for every people has its strengths and its weaknesses. But let me say what I think are our American strengths.

First, we are at our best when we are as natural as our landscape. Whenever we try to be different from our natural selves, from what we really are, we begin to look ridiculous. We are not an old people, and we cannot take on the ways of the old peoples without seeming artificial. That smoothness of finish which is so natural to European peoples, that haughtiness which is essential to the so-called "upper class," simply make us look silly. We Americans are like natural rock. Our glory and our strength are in our naturalness; in saying what we think, unashamed, in doing what we feel is right, unafraid. There is no more reason for us to be ashamed of what we are, than for a column of unhewn granite to be ashamed because it is not a polished diamond. The granite has all its own strength and beauty.

This naturalness, which is our greatest asset, leaves us when we try to be subtle. The only time when I feel slightly ashamed of my countrymen is when one of us tries to be subtle and diplomatic, to cope with those older peoples abroad who are subtle and diplomatic and from old age. It is like a young strong man trying to pretend he is old and cynical and wise. When a young man does that, he loses his own real strength, which is to *be* young, to *be* strong, to take pride in his youth and strength. The old man has not the young man's strength and he resorts to his own compensations for it. But the young man is at his best when he is what he is.

Now, therefore, at this moment in our history, when for the first time we are coming to our full place in the world, let us remember that our American strength is in our youth and naturalness. We do not know how to play politics among the far older politicians of other countries. Those old politicians only smile when they watch us trying to play their game, like old card sharps watching a boy at his first real game of cards. But they are afraid of us when we cut across politics with the demand for reality, for truth-telling, and simplicity, those things in which we are strong because we can be, because we dare to be.

I am proud of our plainness. We are a plain people. We hate false fashionableness and high-hatting, and what we so eloquently call "dog." I was once trying to explain the slang use of that word "dog" to a very old Chinese gentleman, a gentleman so old that he was far beyond any false notions of sophistication and cynicism. Perhaps it is only the half-old people who are very sophisticated and cynical anyway. The Chinese and the Indians are not. And—of course—"dog" is a very American word. I believe it was first used by an American in 1871 to mean "style," or "splurge." It was not used outside of America until the first world war, when our soldiers took it to England, and thence it went to Australia.

WHAT AMERICA MEANS TO ME

"Dog?" my old Chinese gentleman repeated, puzzled. To him the word meant only the animal—*kou* as he called it in Chinese.

"I think it means to act like a big dog among a lot of little ones," I explained.

He was a stout old gentleman and at that moment, it being winter, he was enveloped in many layers of silk-padded robes. Then from out of the middle of that mountain of man I heard a rumble begin and soon he shook with laughter.

"Dog!" he said again, "Dog!—Yes. Wait until I tell that to my new daughter-in-law, just out of college. She thinks she knows more than I do. What is the word for female dog?"

"No, no," I said hastily, "that is something else again."

As it happened, "dog" was good enough, for the young lady had been educated in America and was perfectly able to understand what the old gentleman meant.

It is our plainness that makes the other people of the world like us and trust us—the great plain peoples, the Russians, and the Chinese and the Indians, the peoples who are so old that they can see through all pretenses. We shall hold our own with those peoples, who are far more than half the people in the world, as long as we are our plain selves.

I am proud of our forthrightness. Whenever our leaders have, in the course of our history, cut across the tangle of complexities, put out by lesser men to obscure the issues, whenever our leaders have dared to be forthright and outspoken, our whole nation has risen to new strength.

In 1776, in the midst of complexities greater than we have now, greater because we were so small and weak

WHAT AMERICA MEANS TO ME

and because we faced powers so much stronger than we were, and faced division in our own country, too, far greater than we now have, at that time our leaders, deciding for freedom, gathered behind them all true Americans.

"But when," the Declaration of Independence said, "in a long train of abuses and usurpations, pursuing inevitably the same object, evidence a design to reduce them"—that is, the people—"under absolute Despotism, it is their right, it is their duty, to throw off such Government, and to provide new guards for their future security."

We won that war for freedom, because in spite of difficulties and complexities, we came out with simplicity and forthrightness. We were ourselves, the plain people, the people of America.

In 1864 Abraham Lincoln, that plain American, cutting across the tangles of defeats and disunities, said these clear and forthright words:

> Now, therefore, I, Abraham Lincoln, President of the United States, by virtue of the power in me vested as commander in chief of the army and navy of the United States, in time of actual armed rebellion against the authority and Government of the United States, and as a fit and necessary war measure for suppressing said rebellion . . . do order and declare that all persons held as slaves within said designated States and parts of States are and henceforward shall be free.

By these two declarations for freedom, each taken in times of great national distress and confusions, our people regained their true being and strode forward to win the wars in which they were entangled.

Now we are entangled in international confusion. We

WHAT AMERICA MEANS TO ME

fight this war knowing that it must be fought. But we can win it only by using our own true force, by speaking out plainly against old-world politics and old-world dissensions in our plain American forthright way.

The time has come again to speak for freedom, this time not only for ourselves, not only for people enslaved in our own country. The world has grown far smaller today than even our country was in the days when those two earlier freedoms were declared. We are nearer to India than our eastern states were in those days to our own west coast, and much nearer. We are nearer to China. Today the world waits for a clear simple plain declaration for the freedom of *all* peoples, spoken in a plain American voice.

I am proud because we are a friendly people. All over the world, wherever ordinary Americans have traveled—not diplomats and big business men, but just the ordinary Americans—we have left behind us a warm afterglow of friendly feeling. The Chinese people like our people because we are friendly by nature. We like human beings and we love a joke. The stories that are coming back to us now from India, for example, are heart-warming stories. Our American boys are showing the people of India a new kind of white man—a white man who is a plain human being before he is a soldier or an official. Our American boys don't have to bother to uphold any traditions of Empire and of the white man as ruler, and all that, and in their hours off duty, they are having a good time playing with Indian children and making friends with whoever happens to be around. Maybe you have heard some of the stories about our boys in India. The one I like best is that one which someone tells about having seen a bunch of them out riksha-riding and having seen some of them take a riksha coolie and put him in his own riksha while they pulled him, just for fun. Well, you need to know what a riksha coolie is before you can really appreciate that story. They are the poorest, the most ill-fed, the most hard-worked of human creatures. I can just see that Indian coolie—half-starved, so thin that his naked black legs look spidery, feverishly anxious to do a good job and please the American so as to get a scrap more pay, sweating and mopping himself with a rag, his wretched garments flying behind him as he runs. I don't suppose he ever was pulled in a riksha in his life, and certainly he never sat in his own. And I suppose he was a little frightened when our boys yelled at him, "Hey, you!" He is used to blows and kicks from white men. And then they push him into his riksha and he has to sit down on that cotton-covered cushion he tries to keep clean and inviting for passengers, and before he knows it the merry gang of boys is pulling him along the street, laughing and yelling, and everybody stares for a minute and then they begin to laugh and he begins to laugh and he sees it is all a joke, and perhaps for the first time in his life he realizes that there are white men with whom he can laugh and of whom he need not be afraid because they don't want to be his masters, and when it is all over they pay him the regular fare as if he had pulled them, and for him, forever after, Americans are friendly people.

This precious quality, this great quality of our people, the power of human understanding which makes us a friendly people, must never be lost. It must never be lost through the ambitions of a few men to make America into a new imperialist power. We must fight, as we

WHAT AMERICA MEANS TO ME

fight the Germans and the Japanese, our own ambitious men who would make of America a country to be feared and hated by those who want to be free.

This war is more than a war against the Axis. It is a war against any who would destroy us. The Axis would destroy us, and so we must fight the Axis. But the fascism of the Axis is only part of an evil thing that must not grow in the world. Fascism lurks everywhere like the hidden germs of a deadly disease. It hides in places where we least suspect it. There are germ-carriers of fascism in every nation. Those who harbor race-prejudices are germ carriers of fascism. Those who would build up a great international power of business in the hands of the few at the expense of the people are germ-carriers of fascism. Those who dream of America as the next great imperialist power are germ-carriers of fascism. All who secretly or openly scorn the rights of human beings are germ-carriers of fascism. It is these whom we must discover and deprive of their power.

Can we do it? We must and we can. For I am proud that here in America, our country, we are not only the most democratic people in the world, the most honestly forthright, the most friendly, but we have out of this democratic nature of our people, out of our real passion for fair play, a democratic form of government, in which we the people can, if we will, insist on American ways of thought and behavior. We who are the people have the tools of democracy in our hands. We can control our government. We have our ways of doing it. We choose our leaders and are led by them only so long as they truly represent us. We have the right of free speech, and that means the right of open criticism. We can tell

WHAT AMERICA MEANS TO ME

our leaders what we think, and this can happen in only a very few countries in the world today. We can tell anybody what we think.

One of the things in my life which brings me comfort, these days, is that my mail, for example, is crowded with letters from people I do not know and will probably never know, people from all over America. What do they write to me for? Why, simply to tell me that they like or don't like something I have said or written. They divide fairly evenly between approval and disapproval, but the point is not whether they approve. The point is that they take it as their right to tell me straight what they think. And they have that right, just as I have the right to speak or write in the first place. We all have the right to speak as we think, and we have the right to denounce or uphold our leaders and each other.

It is the most glorious right in the world, for it means that the people in our country have freedom from fear, because we are a free people. We are not ruled by a foreign government, or by a political system which forbids the plain people to speak aloud. We govern ourselves through those whom we choose and we are not subject to them, but they to us.

We must never forget this. The only real danger to our country is from within, that we forget our own power to be what we want to be. Let no American today take refuge in resignation, in that state of willful helplessness which shrugs its shoulders and says, "What can *I* do?" We have the right and the power to make our country what we want it to be. We are the kind of people that democracy produces—free, independent in our thought and behavior, fearless, forthright, and kind. I have seen many peoples of the earth, and it is not only patriotism, I think, when I say that we possess these qualities to a greater degree than any other people. It is not boasting when I say this, for, like a child born with great gifts, we have these qualities not by any effort of ours, but bestowed upon us by our ancestors, by those brave men and women who came here from other lands because freedom was essential to them—the freedom to worship God as they willed, the freedom to work and keep themselves and their families from want, the freedom to believe and to speak as they believed, the freedom to live unafraid, and at peace, beneath the open sky.

We who are the children of these people who gathered here from over all the earth, from many nations and many races, to build a new country, which should be the land of the free, must today march on to fuller freedom. Our great strides have always been taken in the cause of freedom—freedom from empire first, freedom from slavery second, and now it must be the third and greatest freedom for which we fight—the freedom of all mankind.

There is a man who can say better than I can what now ought to be said to you, to all of us who are Americans. He is an American, a high-ranking officer in the United States Marines, but a very plain man. He has led his men in battle with conspicuous bravery. I believe he killed many of the enemy with his own hand. But this did not brutalize him as you will see from these letters. I want to read you two letters he wrote recently.

The first is to the father of one of his men who was killed in action:

WHAT AMERICA MEANS TO ME

My dear Mr. ———:

It is with deep sympathy that I inform you of the death of your son on December the 5th at Guadalcanal, of wounds received in action against the enemy on the fourth of December.

He was a grand youngster. He entered into the spirit and activities of this organization with enthusiastic vigor. His cheerful personality and his unwavering devotion to duty made him a favorite with all with whom he came into contact. I saw him frequently during our recent campaign on Guadalcanal and came to have a great admiration for his fortitude and courage.

He was wounded when he went out as a member of a flanking party against a group of the enemy that had engaged us back in the jungle. He was wounded by machine gun fire. We carried him down the mountain to our lines. I remember going to him at the time and finding him cheerful and smiling. When he was placed in the ambulance I talked with him again. He still wore his cheery smile and assured me that he was all right. On the following day he was placed on the operating table. I am told that he asked the doctors if he might talk. "Better not," they said. "Well," he replied, "I just want to say this: I am proud of this wound and I'm proud of the outfit I'm in. Gosh, we've killed a lot of Japs back there." He failed to survive the operation.

From the above remark you can judge why we of this organization rate him as one of our top heroes. He had what it takes to win this war, and I can assure you that we intend to do all in our power to the end that his sacrifice shall not have been made in vain.

The second letter I received only a few days ago, for this officer is a personal friend. He said he wanted to say something to me, as he put it, "before we steam out again, to meet what lies beyond:"

WHAT AMERICA MEANS TO ME

It is not the outcome of the war that stirs my apprehension. It is the justifiable fear that victory will not bring realization of the peace and freedom for which we fight; that type of peace and freedom which is consonant with our democratic ideals, which statesmen so lustily proclaim—and then deny in their acts. This fear hangs over me like a pall. It hangs over the heads of all honest men who live in the presence of death, that the final victory may be ours. The presence of this fear has the inevitable effect of impairing the enthusiasm with which we attack our job. It can be dissipated only by the knowledge that our statesmen are honestly endeavoring to bring into universal living reality these principles of freedom which have brought renewed hope to mankind and which alone can cement mutual confidence and understanding among nations.

A few days ago at one of our battalion forums I spoke to my men of my fear that the things for which they now fight can be attained only by a struggle at home after the Axis powers have been subdued. I found that my words struck a responsive chord. These men are far from being stupid. They will not, like their fathers, acquiesce in the efforts of short-sighted leaders to maintain the status quo. They have a well-defined conception of what freedom means and I am confident that they will insist, even fight, that it be something more than a mere conception.

I hope you will continue to prod people into realizing that the power to shape patterns and objectives is theirs, and that unless they shed their lethargy and assume the obligation as their own the sacrifices they are now making will have been in vain.

There are brave men fighting for us on the battle front, but we, too, are on the battle front. Here, in field and factory, in homes, in schools, everywhere throughout our land, we are embattled in the same cause, to rid ourselves and our country, and with us all mankind, of the

WHAT AMERICA MEANS TO ME

black threat of fear from those who deny the right of peoples to be free. This war is our war. We must win it, for if we lost it we would lose all that we hold most dear. This American earth would be no more valuable than any other if upon it we could not live in freedom.

We have everything for which to fight—America, our own country, founded in freedom, grown great in freedom; our people, the most fortunate on earth, not because we are rich but because we are free. We have everything with which to win—we have in our own hands the tools to keep our freedom and to make the kind of life that human beings should have. We can do what we will. We are Americans.